The Star Clippers'
Gracious Writ

On the Partaking in a Voyage aboard a Tall Ship

Name - Name - Nom

Departure from - Abfahrt von - Départ de

Port of Call - Anlaufhafen - Port d'escale

Name of Ship - Name des Schiffes - Nom du voilier

Date - Datum - Date

Master - Kapitän - Capitaine

The Star Clipper Saga

And the Glorious Era of the Clipper Ships

by Erling Matz

Contents

In 1849 gold was found in California and in 1851 gold was found in Australia. This triggered off the "Gold Rush". At this time, and up until 1869, the ultimate tool for intercontinental transportation was the sailing ship. Suddenly speed meant money and the famous Clipper Ships, the most beautiful and fastest sailing ships that ever crossed the oceans, were developed.

I was fortunate enough to grow up in the Stockholm archipelago by the Baltic Sea. Nearby my home was one of the world's finest yacht building yards where I spent a lot of my time as a small boy.

Whenever a fabulous new yacht was launched I heard the workers say:

"She'll sail like a McKay Clipper".

It took me some years to understand that they were referring to Donald McKay, sometimes called the Father of the Clipper ships (more about him later in this book).

While my class mates admired football stars, my hero was Donald McKay, and as a small boy I made him a solemn promise one day to put those Clippers ships back on the ocean.

Im Jahre 1849 wurde in Kalifornien Gold gefunden und 1851 in Australien. Dies löste den Goldrausch aus. Zu dieser Zeit und bis 1869 war das Segelschiff die ausschließliche Form des internationalen Güterverkehrs. Plötzlich hieß es, Zeit ist Geld und die berühmten Klipperschiffe wurden entwickelt, die schönsten und schnellsten Segelschiffe, die je die Ozeane überquerten.

Ich hatte das Glück in den Schären von Stockholm aufzuwachsen. Nicht weit von meinem Elternhaus befand sich eine der besten Werften für den Bau von Yachten. Als kleiner Junge verbrachte ich dort viel Zeit. Immer wenn eine neue wundervolle Yacht vom Stapel lief, hörte ich die Arbeiter sagen: „Sie wird segeln wie ein McKay Klipper". Es brauchte ein paar Jahre, bis ich verstand, dass sie von Donald McKay sprachen, der manchmal als Vater der Klipperschiffe bezeichnet wird.

Während meine Klassenkameraden Fußballstars bewunderten, war mein Held Donald McKay und als kleiner Junge machte ich ihm das heilige Versprechen, eines Tages die Klipperschiffe wieder auf die Ozeane zu bringen.

En 1849 de l'or fût découvert en Californie et en 1851 en Australie. Ceci a déclenché la « Ruée vers l'Or ». A cette époque, et jusqu'en 1869, le transport international était fait par les bateaux à voile. Subitement, la vitesse est liée à l'argent et les fameux Voiliers Clippers, les plus beaux et les plus rapides voiliers qui n'aient jamais traversé les océans, ont été développés.

J'ai eu la chance de grandir dans l'archipel de Stockholm en mer Baltique. A côté de ma maison, il y avait l'un des meilleurs chantiers navals dans lequel j'ai passé beaucoup de temps quand j'étais un petit garçon. Chaque fois qu'un nouveau et fabuleux yacht était mis à l'eau, j'entendais les ouvriers dire : « Il naviguera comme le Clipper de McKay ». Cela m'a pris bien des années pour comprendre qu'ils se référaient à Donald McKay, que l'on nommait quelque fois le Père des voiliers Clipper.

Pendant que mes camarades de classe admiraient les stars du football, mon héros était Donald McKay. En tant que petit garçon je lui fis la promesse solennelle que je remettrai ces Clippers à nouveau sur l'océan.

Mikael Krafft
Managing Owner Star Clippers

YESTERDAY

In 1902, the world's first five-masted full-rigger was built - the *Preussen*. "Those who saw it were rendered speechless", wrote the well-known British maritime historian Alan Villiers. 98 years would pass, before another five-masted full-rigger was built - the *Royal Clipper*.

GESTERN

1902 wurde das erste Fünfmastvollschiff der Welt gebaut - die *Preußen*. „Wer immer sie sah, war sprachlos", schrieb der bekannte britische Maritimhistoriker Alan Villiers. 98 Jahre sollten vergehen bis ein zweites Fünfmastvollschiff gebaut wurde - die *Royal Clipper*.

HIER

En 1902, le premier cinq mâts carré fût construit - le *Preussen*. « Ceux qui l'ont vus sont restés muets d'admiration » , écrivit l'historien britannique bien connu Alan Villiers. Il a fallu 98 ans pour qu'un autre cinq mâts carré soit construit - le *Royal Clipper*.

TODAY

The five-masted full-rigger *Preussen* inspired Mikael Krafft, owner of Star Clippers, to have the *Royal Clipper* built – the world's second five-masted full-rigger. The *Royal Clipper* has a length of 134 metres (439 ft) and carries 5,050 sq. metres (54,300 sq. ft) of sail.

HEUTE

Der Fünfmaster *Preußen* inspirierte Mikael Krafft, Eigentümer von Star Clippers, die *Royal Clipper* bauen zu lassen - das zweite Fünfmastvollschiff. Die *Royal Clipper* hat eine Länge von 134 Metern und eine Segelfläche von 5,050 m².

AUJOURD'HUI

Inspiré par le cinq mâts *Preussen* Mikael Krafft, propriétaire et fondateur de Star Clippers, décida de construire le *Royal Clipper*, le deuxième cinq mâts carré au monde jamais construit. Le *Royal Clipper* a une longueur de 134 mètres et compte 5 050 m² de voiles.

TODAY

Polyester fibres are used for sails and ropes. The sails retain their shape better, they are stronger and do not get spoiled by moisture. But they are still subject to wear. Just like in the old sailing ship days, sails and ropes always have to be looked after on the Star Clipper ships.

HEUTE

Segel und Seile bestehen aus Polyester-fasern. Die Segel behalten ihre Form, sind stärker und werden nicht durch Feuchtig-keit beschädigt. Sie leiden aber immer noch unter Abnutzung. Wie in den alten Zeiten der Segelschiffe müssen auch heute die Segel und Seile auf den Star Clipper Schiffen ständig überwacht werden.

AUJOURD'HUI

Les fibres en polyester sont utilisées pour les voiles et les cordages. Mais elles sont toujours sujettes à l'usure. Juste comme au temps des vieux voiliers, les voiles et les cordages doivent être toujours vérifiés sur les bateaux de Star Clippers.

YESTERDAY

Sails and ropes were usually made of hemp. There were several thicknesses of canvas, the heaviest for the stormy waters around Cape Horn, and the thinnest for the light winds near the Equator. Repairing sails and making new ones was a never-ending task on board.

GESTERN

Segel und Seile wurden üblicherweise aus Hanf hergestellt. Es gab mehrere Stärken für Segeltuch, die schwersten für die stürmische See um Kap Horn und die leichtesten für die schwachen Winde nahe am Äquator. Segelreparaturen und Herstellung neuer Segel waren eine ständige Aufgabe an Bord.

HIER

Les voiles et les cordages sont faits habituel-lement de chanvre. Il y avait plusieurs épaisseurs de voile; les plus solides pour les tempêtes autour du Cap Horn et les plus légères pour les vents faibles autour de l'Equateur. Réparer les voiles et en fabri-quer de nouvelles était un travail sans fin à bord.

YESTERDAY

Capstans were used in the old clipper ships for weighing anchor and hoisting heavy sails. Many hands were needed to man the capstan. In the late 1880s, small steam engines were introduced for the heaviest tasks on board, and crew numbers could be reduced.

GESTERN

Auf den alten Klipperschiffen lichtete man den Anker und hisste die schweren Segel mit dem Gangspill. Viele Matrosen mussten das Gangspill bedienen. In den achtziger Jahren des neunzehnten Jahrhunderts wurden kleine Dampfmaschinen eingeführt, um die schwersten Arbeiten an Bord auszuführen. Damit konnte die Zahl der Besatzungsmitglieder verringert werden.

HIER

Des cabestans étaient utilisés par les anciens Clippers pour soulever l'ancre et hisser les lourdes voiles. De nombreux bras étaient nécessaires pour les tourner. A la fin des années 1880, de petits moteurs à vapeur ont été installés pour les bateaux les plus lourds, et ainsi, l'équipage pouvait être limité.

TODAY

On the Star Clipper ships, electrical winches are used for handling the sails. But still, many kilometres of rope have to be handled. The miles of rope that form the rigging of a sailing vessel demand many different knots, splices and seizings. A knot should have the following properties: It must hold. It should cause as little wear as possible on the rope. It must be easy to tie. It must be easy to untie. It should preferably look beautiful and harmonious.

HEUTE

Auf den Star Clipper Schiffen werden die Segel mit elektrischen Winden bewegt. Aber immer noch müssen viele Kilometer an Seilen bedient werden. Die kilometerlangen Seile auf einem Segelschiff erfordern eine Menge verschiedener Knoten und Spleiße. Ein Knoten sollte die folgenden Eigenschaften haben: Er muss halten. Er sollte die Festigkeit des Seiles so wenig wie möglich beeinträchtigen. Er muss leicht zu knüpfen und leicht zu lösen sein. Er sollte möglichst gut und harmonisch aussehen.

AUJOURD'HUI

Sur les voiliers de Star Clippers, des winches électriques sont utilisés pour établir les voiles. Mais il y a encore de nombreux kilomètres de cordages à manipuler. Les marins utilisent des kilomètres de cordage et différents types de nœuds pour le gréement des bateaux. Un nœud devra avoir les propriétés suivantes: Il doit tenir. Il doit aussi causer aussi peu de dommage que possible au cordage. Il doit être facile à défaire. De préférence, il doit être beau et harmonieux.

YESTERDAY

It was important always to keep a lookout. In good visibility, a lookout standing on deck can see four nautical miles (7 400 metres), before land or a ship starts to disappear below the horizon. From twenty metres (65 ft) up in the mast, the visibility range is twice as long.

GESTERN

Es war und ist immer wichtig, einen Ausguck zu haben. Bei guter Sicht konnte ein Ausguck auf Deck vier nautische Meilen (7400 Meter) weit sehen, bevor Land oder ein Schiff unter dem Horizont verschwanden. Aus zwanzig Metern Höhe im Mast ist die Sichtweite das Doppelte.

HIER

Il était important de tout surveiller tout autour du navire. Par bonne visibilité depuis le pont, on pouvait voir à quatre mille marin (7400 mètres), avant la côte, ou avant qu'un bateau disparaisse sous l'horizon. A vingt mètres dans le mât, la visibilité est doublée.

TODAY

Two crew members hoist the Star Clipper house flag. Often three flags are flown. The house flag on the mainmast, the national flag (ensign) in the stern and the courtesy flag on the foremast. The courtesy flag is flown by a ship in foreign waters as a token of respect.

HEUTE

Zwei Besatzungsmitglieder hissen die Reedereiflagge von Star Clippers. Oft werden drei Flaggen gezeigt: Die Reedereiflagge an dem Großmast, die Nationalflagge am Heck und die Gast-landflagge an dem Fockmast als Zeichen von Respekt in fremden Gewässern.

AUJOURD'HUI

Deux membres d'équipage hissent le drapeau de la compagnie Star Clippers. Habituellement 3 drapeaux sont hissés. Le pavillon du propriétaire sur le grand mât, le drapeau national sur le mât d'artimon et le pavillon de courtoisie sur le mât de misaine. Le pavillon de courtoisie est hissé par un bateau en eaux étrangères comme une marque de respect.

TODAY

Crossing the Atlantic on a Star Clippers' ship takes about two weeks. Fourteen days of the tranquil movements of a ship under sail, day and night, and with nothing but the horizon around you. Still, there is always something to do - for passengers as well as for crew.

HEUTE

Die Reise über den Atlantik auf einem Star Clippers Schiff dauert ungefähr zwei Wochen. Vierzehn Tage mit der beruhigenden Bewegung eines Schiffes unter Segel, Tag und Nacht und nichts mehr als den Horizont in Sicht. Trotzdem, es gibt immer etwas zu tun - für Passagiere wie auch für die Besatzung.

AUJOURD'HUI

Il faut environ deux semaines pour un voilier de Star Clippers pour traverser l'Atlantique. Quatorze jours de mouvements tranquilles pour un voilier sous voile, jour et nuit, rien autour de vous sinon l'horizon. Mais il y a toujours quelque chose à faire pour les passagers aussi bien que pour l'équipage.

YESTERDAY

Three, four months at sea without entering a port. Everything on board had to be managed by the ship's crew. Sewing sails and repairing rigging and hull and many other things. Here, a makeshift smithy has been set up on the four-masted barque *Beatrice*.

GESTERN

Drei, vier Monate auf See ohne einen Hafen anzulaufen. Alles an Bord des Schiffes musste von der Besatzung erledigt werden, Nähen von Segeln, Reparatur von Seilen, Takelage, Schiffsrumpf und viele andere Dinge. Hier ist eine provisorische Schmiede auf der Viermastbark *Beatrice* zu sehen.

HIER

Trois, quatre mois en mer sans mettre pied à terre. Chaque chose à bord doit être gerée par l'équipage du bateau. Réparer les voiles, le gréement, la coque et beaucoup d'autres choses. Ici, une forge de fortune a été mise en place sur la barque quatre-mâts *Beatrice*.

Too Late
Just in Time

THE LAST VOYAGES *with cargo in square-riggers took place in the late 1940's. But the romance of sailing ships lived on. Forty years later, Mikael Krafft (photo) had an idea.*

DIE FAHRTEN *der Großsegler mit Ladung endeten gegen Ende der Vierziger Jahre des letzten Jahrhunderts. Die Romantik der Segelschiffe lebte jedoch weiter. Vierzig Jahre später hatte Mikael Krafft (Foto) eine Idee.*

LES DERNIERS VOYAGES *avec des voiliers transporteurs de marchandises à voiles carrées ont eu lieu à la fin des années 1940. Mais la romance des voiliers existe encore. Quarante ans plus tard Mikael Krafft (photo) eut une idée.*

THE STOCKHOLM *cinema was called Vinterpalatset - "Winter Palace".*

DAS KINO *in Stockholm hatte den Namen Vinterpalatset - „Winterpalast".*

LE CINÉMA *de Stockholm était appelé Vinterpalatset - « Palais d'hiver ».*

t is not known who in 1958 invented the word Cinemiracle. But a cinematic miracle it was. The screen was a harmonious curve, measuring 100 by 40 feet. Three simultaneous projectors filled the screen. And the sound was played in seven channel HiFi. Everything was new and miraculous. In fastidious Hollywood, the film Windjammer ran for 36 weeks. In less fastidious Sweden, it ran for 100 weeks - and every evening to full houses. The Stockholm cinema was called Vinterpalatset ("Winter Palace"). It was built specially for this film, where the main character was not a seductive woman or a brave man, but a beautiful ship - the Norwegian full-rigger *Christian Radich*. The opening was on September 4, 1958. Mikael Krafft was 12 years old, and he still remembers:

"The first 15 minutes were shown in the usual format and in black-and-white. Then, the screen suddenly widened, the ship put to sea and set sails and the strings and brass of the Boston Pops Orchestra filled the theatre." It was unabashed sailing ship romance and the producer was right. Millions of people succumbed. Even today, the film is discussed on internet forums and many are those who remember it and hope to see it again:

"I'm thrilled to learn my dream of seeing this film again may come true! Saw it at the age of 5", writes the signature Vidiot, and immediately receives a reply with all about the film and its unique technique.

Mikael Krafft, owner of Star Clippers, also remembers. Already as a young boy, he was in love with sailing ships. So much in love that at 12 years old he sailed to Åland, just to see and be close to the four-master barque *Pommern*, a museum ship in Mariehamn. A 12-year old who, without the knowledge of his parents takes his little wooden sailboat and sails seventy nautical miles - 23 of which were on the open sea - is madly in love or just mad. Probably both.

On arrival, young Mikael was not satisfied by merely looking at the *Pommern*. He climbed up the rigging - also without permission. A guard caught sight of him and yelled: "Come on down!!! If you don't, you'll fall down and kill yourself. But I'll kill you anyway when you come down."

Mikael Krafft survived, and that was the beginning of the Star Clipper saga.

WINDJAMMER A CINEMIRACLE

Windjammer - ein Filmwunder. Man weiß nicht, wer 1958 das Wort Cinemiracle erfand, aber für die Filmtechnik war es ein wahres Wunder. Die Filmleinwand hatte eine harmonische Krümmung mit den Maßen 100 x 40 Fuß. Drei simultane Projektoren füllten die Leinwand und der Ton spielte auf sieben HiFi Kanälen. Alles war neu und wie ein Wunder. Im wählerischen Hollywood lief der Film Windjammer für 36 Wochen, im weniger verwöhnten Schweden für 100 Wochen und jeden Abend vor vollem Haus. Das Kino war speziell für diesen Film gebaut worden, in dem nicht eine verführerische Frau oder ein kühner Mann die Hauptrolle spielten, sondern ein schönes Schiff - der norwegische Großsegler *Christian Radich*. Die Premiere war am 4. September 1958. Mikael Krafft, Eigentümer der Reederei Star Clippers, war 12 Jahre alt und erinnert sich noch:

„Die ersten 15 Minuten wurden im üblichen Format und in schwarzweiß gezeigt. Dann erweiterte sich plötzlich die Leinwand, das Schiff legte ab und setzte Segel. Das war die Freiheit! Die Streich- und Blasinstrumente des Boston Pops Orchesters brachten den Saal über sieben Kanäle zum vibrieren. Das war reine Segel-romantik ohne die geringste Zurückhaltung, und der Produzent sollte recht behalten."

Millionen von Menschen waren mitgerissen. Noch heute wird der Film im Internet diskutiert: „Ich bin begeistert zu hören, dass ich diesen Film vielleicht noch einmal erleben kann! Ich sah ihn im Alter von fünf Jahren", schreibt jemand mit der Unterschrift Vidiot und erhält sofort eine Antwort mit allen Einzelheiten über den Film und dessen einzigartige Technik.

Mikael Krafft erinnert sich ebenso. Schon als Jugendlicher war er fasziniert von Segelschiffen. So fasziniert, dass er nach Åland segelte, nur um die Viermastbark *Pommern* zu sehen und in ihre Nähe zu kommen. Sie ist als Museumsschiff in Mariehamn vertäut. Ein 12jähriger, der ohne Wissen seiner Eltern mit seinem kleinen hölzernen Segelboot allein 70 Seemeilen davon 23 über offenes Meer segelt, muss völlig vernarrt sein oder verrückt; wahrscheinlich beides. Einmal angekommen, war der junge Mikael natürlich nicht damit zufrieden, die *Pommern* nur anzusehen. Er kletterte hoch in die Takelage, ebenso ohne Erlaubnis. Ein Wächter, der ihn entdeckte, schrie: „Komm sofort herunter, wenn du nicht fällst und dich selbst umbringst, bringe ich dich sowieso um, wenn du herunterkommst."

Mikael Krafft überlebte und damit begann die einzigartige Geschichte von Star Clippers.

L'histoire ne révèle pas le nom de celui qui inventa le mot « cinemiracle », mais il s'agissait bel et bien d'un miracle du 7éme art. L'écran était une courbe harmonieuse, mesurant 100 par 40 pieds. Trois projecteurs éclairaient simultanément l'écran et le son émanait de sept chaînes HiFi. Tout était nouveau et miraculeux. A Hollywood, le film fut projeté dans les salles pendant 36 semaines. En Suède, où le public était beaucoup moins cinéphile, il fut projeté pendant 100 semaines - et chaque soir la salle était comble. Elle a été spécialement construite pour ce film, où le sujet principal n'était pas une femme séductrice ou un brave homme, mais un magnifique bateau - le trois-mâts carré norvégien *Christian Radich*.

La première a eu lieu le 4 septembre 1958. Mikael Krafft, propriétaire de Star Clippers, avait 12 ans et s'en souvient encore:

« Les premières 15 minutes étaient dans le format normal et en noir et blanc. Puis l'écran s'agrandit, la mer sembla tout près, le bateau hissa les voiles et prit le large accompagné de la musique de l'orchestre des « Boston Pops ». Il y avait un vrai sentiment de liberté et d'aventure. Certes le réalisateur avait prit un gros risque, mais il avait vu juste. Des millions de gens y succombèrent. » Même aujourd'hui, le film fait l'objet de discussions sur des forums internet et nombreux sont ceux qui s'en souviennent et espèrent le revoir.

« Je suis râvi d'apprendre que mon rêve de revoir ce film devient réel ! Vu à l'âge de 5 ans », écrit le signataire Vidiot qui reçut immédiatement une réponse sur tout à propos du film et sa technique unique.

Mikael Krafft s'en souvient aussi. Dès son plus jeune âge, il tomba amoureux des bateaux à voile. Tellement amoureux qu'il naviga jusqu'à Åland, juste pour voir et être près du quatre-mâts barque, le *Pommern*. La même année, il était amarré pour toujours, comme bateau musée à Mariehamn. Un garçon de 12 ans qui, sans l'aide de ses parents prend son petit voilier en bois et navigue soixantedix milles nautiques - dont 23 au large - est, soit follement amoureux, ou juste fou. Probablement les deux.

A son arrivée, le jeune Mikael n'était pas satisfait de regarder seulement le *Pommern*. Il grimpa en haut du gréement, sans permission. Un garde l'interpella et hurla :

« Descends !!! Sinon tu tomberas et tu te tueras. Mais je te tuerai de toute façon quand tu seras descendu. »

Mikael Krafft survécu, et c'était le début de la saga de Star Clippers.

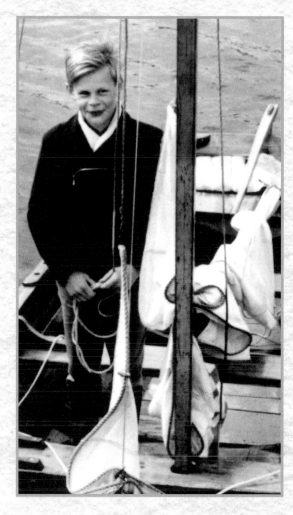

YOUNG Mikael Krafft and his little sailing boat.

DER JUNGE Mikael Krafft und sein kleines Holzsegelboot.

LE JEUNE Mikael Krafft et son petit bateau à voile.

A SELF-WILLED SWEDE

Serendipity is the scientific term. The easy translation is "pleasant surprise". The American physician Julius H. Comroe once stated it as "To look for a needle in a haystack and get out of it with the farmer's daughter". In 1987, Mikael Krafft was struck:

"We were on board my yacht *Gloria*, a 190 ton staysail schooner and were anchored, as I remember, on a very warm winter's evening just off the coast of St. Martin. It was one of the tropical nights, you know, when the sun was just dipping into the ocean and gentle trade winds were wafting through the yard-arms. Suddenly all the pieces seemed to come together - like a light going through my brain."

The pieces were: • The wonderful sailing trips in his youth among the 28,000 islands of the Stockholm archipelago. • His single-handed sailing to Åland in 1958. • His knowledge about the most beautiful and the speediest ships ever built - the clippers of the 19th century. • His cruises with his own yachts. Serendipity!

"I decided to build a genuine large sailing ship, with the wind as the most important source of power. No one had done that for almost a hundred years. The ship should resemble old clippers in hull but with a stern like my *Gloria*, yet be designed to accommodate some 150 guests. In my new clipper, I wanted to include all the romance of sail and style that you find in a large sailing yacht, such as those that I have been lucky enough to sail. Softly varnished maroon mahogany and warm yellow brass. There, at the anchorage in the lee of St. Martin, I wanted others to share this with me."

After four years and seven sorrows, the *Star Flyer* was launched in Ghent, Belgium, 1991. In 1992, her sister ship *Star Clipper* was launched, and in 2000 the five-masted full-rigger *Royal Clipper*. And the seven sorrows?

"First and foremost, it was a question of adjusting a genuine sailing ship to all modern security regulations. No ship like the *Star Flyer* had been built for almost 100 years, and that was before the sinking of the *Titanic* in 1912. That frightful accident led to changes in all rules concerning stability and a great many other things."

Adjusting this to modern sailing was the "seven sorrows" of the Bible, but it succeeded.

Im Englischen gibt es den Ausdruck *serendipity*. Vereinfacht wird er mit „freudige Überraschung" übersetzt. Der amerikanische Arzt Julius H. Comroe formulierte das einmal so: „Nach einer Nadel im Heuhaufen suchen und mit der Tochter des Farmers herauskommen".

Im Jahre 1987 überkam es Mikael Krafft: „Wir waren an Bord meiner Yacht *Gloria*, ein 190 Tonnen Stagsegel Schoner, und ich erinnere mich, dass wir an einem warmen Winter abend bei St. Martin vor Anker lagen. Es war eine dieser tropischen Nächte. Die Sonne versank gerade im Ozean und eine leichte Brise wehte durch die Takelage. Plötzlich schienen alle Einzelheiten zusammenzukommen - als wenn ein Funke durch meinen Kopf ging."

Die Einzelheiten waren: • Die wundervollen Segeltouren seiner Jugend zwischen den 28 000 Inseln im Archipel von Stockholm. • Seine Reise nach Åland allein im Segelboot im Jahre 1958. • Sein Wissen über die Klipper des 19. Jahrhunderts. • Die Segeltörns mit seinen eigenen Yachten. Serendipity!

"Ich beschloss, ein echtes grosses Segelschiff zu bauen, mit dem Wind als wichtigste Antriebsquelle. Seit fast hundert Jahren hatte das niemand mehr getan. Das Schiff sollte den alten Klippern in Schiffsrumpf, Rigg und Verhalten im Wasser gleichen und das Achterschiff wie meine *Gloria*, aber so konstruiert sein, dass es 150 Gäste aufnehmen konnte. In meinem neuen Klipper wollte ich die Segelromantik, den Luxus, Komfort und Stil verwirklichen, den man auf den großen Segelyachten findet, die ich hatte segeln dürfen. Dort, vor Anker im Lee von St. Martin, wollte ich dies mit anderen teilen".

Nach vier Jahren und sieben Plagen, lief die *Star Flyer* in Gent, Belgien, 1991 vom Stapel. Im Jahre 1992 folgte das Schwesterschiff *Star Clipper* und im Jahre 2000 das *Royal Clipper*. Und die sieben Plagen?

Kein Schiff wie die *Star Flyer* war in den vergangenen hundert Jahren gebaut worden. Das letzte Mal vor dem Untergang der *Titanic* im Jahre 1912. Mit diesem schrecklichen Unglück änderten sich alle Regeln für die Stabilität, wasser-dichte Schotten und vieles, vieles anderes. All dieses in ein modernes Segelboot zu integrieren, waren die sieben Plagen, aber es gelang.

Serendipity est le terme scientifique. La traduction la plus facile est « surprise agréable ». Le physicien américain Julius H. Comroe le définit comme « Rechercher une aiguille dans une botte de foin et en sortir avec la fille du fermier ». En 1987, Mikael Krafft vécu l'expérience:

« Nous étions à bord de mon voilier, le *Gloria* une goélette à trinquette de 190 tonneaux, et nous étions ancrés, si je me souviens bien, un soir très chaud juste le long de la côte de Saint Martin. C'était l'une de ces nuits tropicales, vous savez, quand le soleil venait juste de plonger dans l'océan et qu'un vent léger flottait à travers les vergues. Tout à coup toutes les pièces du puzzle semblaient se rassembler comme une lumière traversant mon cerveau. »

Les pièces étaient: • Les sorties merveilleuses à la voile depuis son jeune âge à travers les 20 000 îles de l'archipel de Stockholm. • Sa sortie en solitaire à Åland en 1958. • Sa connaissance des Clippers du 19è siècle. • Ses croisières avec son propre voilier.

Eureka! « Je décidais de construire un grand voilier authentique, avec le vent comme principale source d'énergie. Personne n'avait fait çà depuis près d'une centaine d'années. Le bateau devra ressembler aux vieux clippers par sa coque, son gréement et la manière de se mouvoir sur l'eau et la poupe que j'ai prise depuis mon *Gloria*. Dans mon nouveau clipper, je veux inclure tout le romantisme de la voile, le luxe, le confort et le style que vous trouvez dans un grand voilier, comme ceux avec lesquels j'ai eu la chance de naviguer. Ici à l'ancre sous le vent de Saint Martin, je voudrais que d'autres partagent ceci avec moi. »

Après quatre ans et sept plaies *Star Flyer* fut lancé à Gant en Belgique 1991. En 1992, son bateau-sœur, le *Star Clipper* fut lancé, et en 2000 *Royal Clipper*. Et les sept plaies ? « En tout premier lieu, c'était une question d'ajustement véritable d'un voilier à toutes les lois modernes et aux règles de sécurité. Pas un bateau comme le *Star Flyer* n'avait été construit depuis plus de 100 ans, et cela avant le naufrage du *Titanic* en 1912. Cet accident épouvantable a changé toutes les règles concernant la stabilité et beaucoup d'autres choses. » Adapter ceci à un voilier moderne était les « sept plaies » de la Bible, mais ce fut un succès.

THE WORLD of Mikael Krafft. Stockholm Archipelago. Caribbean sunset. An old windjammer. Painting Star Clipper and Gloria.
© Geoff Hunt PPRSMA

MIKAEL KRAFFTS Welt. Stockholms Schären. Sonnenuntergang in der Karibik. Ein alter Windjammer. Gemälde von Star Clipper und Gloria.
© Geoff Hunt PPRSMA

LE MONDE de Mikael Krafft. L'archipel de Stockholm. Coucher de soleil dans les Caraïbes. Un vieux coureur des mers. Peinture de Star Clipper et Gloria.
© Geoff Hunt PPRSMA

SMALL IS BEAUTIFUL

The harbours that the clippers, and later the square-riggers of the German Laeisz and the Åland Erikson companies, called at were most often small open bays or river mouths. At best, there was a coarsely timbered wooden jetty, nothing else. The ships had to anchor close to the shore to facilitate loading.

Just like the old clipper ships, the ships of Star Clippers sometimes slip into small coves and minor ports. There will rarely be a dilapidated wooden jetty, but otherwise, much is alike. That is a part of the Star Clippers philosophy.

Small is beautiful. That goes for ships, ports and anchorages.

Big cruise ships with thousands of passengers require large ports with quays, terminals and parking areas for sightseeing buses.

If the number of guests on board is 150, or 200, as with Star Clippers, nothing of this is needed. Intimacy is a part of the experience.

Just two of many examples:

Wet Landing on a solitary beach in Costa Rica. The crew sets up a buffet lunch in the shade of the palm trees. Poisson cru - lime marinated tuna - grilled chicken and corn, aubergine, tomatoes, cucumber, beans, lettuce… pineapple, orange, papaya, grapes, pears, apple… beer, wine, water. Not like in the days of the clippers, but as if you were sailing on your own yacht.

Or:

Sail in between precipitous cliffs on southern Corsica. 100 metres high rocks and then discover the little port of Bonifacio. It is a demonstration of seamanship.

The approach is hardly more than a ship's length wide. Then, there is a 90-degree bend. It is also a voyage back in time.

This is where Odysseus sought shelter 3,000 years ago. Yes, he noted the 90-degree bend. He was met by the Laestrygonians. According to Homer, they bombarded the ships with boulders, pelted from the heights, speared his men like fish and devoured them. Eleven of his twelve ships were destroyed.

The reception is different today, and small is beautiful.

Die Klipperschiffe und später die Rahsegler der deutschen Laeisz und der Erikson aus Åland liefen meist kleine Meeresbuchten und Fluss-mündungen an. Im besten Fall gab es einen grob gezimmerten Holzsteg, sonst nichts. Die Schiffe mussten nahe am Ufer ankern, um das Laden und Entladen zu erleichtern.

Genau wie die Klipperschiffe ankert Star Clippers von Zeit zu Zeit in kleine Buchten und kleinere Häfen. Jetzt gibt es nur noch selten einen verfallenen Landungssteg aus Holz, aber sonst ist vieles wie früher. Dies ist ein Teil der Philosophie von Star Clippers. Klein, aber fein, das gilt für Schiff, Hafen und Ankerplatz.

Große Kreuzfahrtschiffe mit tausenden von Passagieren benötigen große Häfen mit Kaianlagen, Terminalen und Parkplätzen für Sightseeing- Busse. Wenn die Anzahl der Gäste an Bord hundertund-fünfzig oder zweihundert beträgt, wie bei Star Clippers, ist nichts dergleichen notwendig. Intimi-tät ist Teil des Erlebnisses. Nur zwei Beispiele von vielen:

Landung an einem einsamen Sandstrand in Costa Rica. Die Besatzung serviert ein Lunch Buffet im Schatten von Palmen: poisson cru - in Limonen marinierter Thunfisch - gegrilltes Hühnchen und Mais, Auberginen, Tomaten, Gurken, Bohnen, Salat … Ananas, Apfelsinen, Papayas, Weintrauben, Bir-nen, Äpfel … Bier, Wein, Wasser. Nicht wie zur Zeit der Klipperschiffe, sondern eher wie bei einem Segeltörn auf der eigenen Yacht.

Oder: Segeln zwischen steilen Klippen im Süden Korsikas. Hundert Meter hohe Felsen und dann den kleinen Hafen Bonifacio entdecken. Dies ist eine Demonstration von seemännischem Geschick. Die Einfahrt ist kaum mehr als eine Bootslänge breit, gefolgt von einer neunzig Grad Wende. Es ist außerdem eine Reise zurück in die Geschichte. An dieser Stelle suchte Odysseus vor 3000 Jahren einen Nothafen. Ja, auch er bemerkte die neunzig Grad Biegung. Hier traf er auf die Lästrygonen. Laut Homer schleuderten sie große Felsbrocken auf die Schiffe, spießten seine Männer auf wie Fische und verschlangen sie. Elf von seinen zwölf Schiffen wurden zerstört. Der Empfang ist heute ganz anders: Klein, aber fein.

Les Clippers et plus tard les voiles carrées appartenant à la compagnie allemande Laeisz et la société Erikson d'Åland utilisaient des « ports » qui n'étaient guère plus que des embouchures de rivière ou des toutes petites baies avec au mieux une jetée grossièrement bâtie en bois, et rien d'autre. Les bateaux devaient ancrer près du rivage pour faciliter le chargement.

Tout comme les Clippers d'antan les bateaux de Star Clippers entrent parfois dans des petites baies et des ports de petite taille. Mais autrement dit, tout est inchangé. Plus c'est petit, plus c'est beau, fait parti de la philosophie de Star Clippers tant pour les bateaux, les ports et les mouillages.

Les grands paquebots avec des milliers de passagers exigent des grands ports avec des quais, des terminaux et des parkings pour les excursions en autocars. Avec 150 ou 200 passagers, comme avec Star Clippers, l'ambiance est forcément conviviale et intimiste.

Seulement deux exemples parmi beaucoup d'autres: Débarquement en chaloupe sur une plage isolée au Costa Rica. L'équipage dresse un buffet pour le déjeuner à l'ombre des palmiers. Poisson cru et thon mariné au citron - poulet grillé et maïs, tomates, aubergines, concombres, petits pois, laitues … ananas, oranges, papaye, raisin, poires, pommes … bière, vin, eau.

Pas comme au temps des clippers, mais comme si vous naviguiez sur votre propre voilier.

Ou: Naviguer entre les falaises escarpées du sud de la Corse. 100 m de hauts rochers avant de découvrir le petit port de Bonifacio. L'approche est à peine plus large que la largeur du bateau. Puis, il y a un virage à 90 degrés. C'est aussi un voyage en retour dans le temps.

C'est là que l'Odyssée recherchait un abri il y a 3000 ans. En effet, il nota le virage de 90 degrés. Il y rencontra les Laestrygoniens.

Selon Homer, ils bombardaient les bateaux avec des blocs de pierre, lancés depuis les hauteurs, transperçaient ses hommes comme des poissons et les dévoraient. Onze de ses douze bateaux furent détruits.

La perception est différente aujourd'hui, plus c'est petit, plus c'est beau.

IN THE NARROW harbour of Syracuse on Sicily.

DER ENGE Hafen von Syrakus.

DANS L'ETROIT port de Siracuse en Sicile.

WE ARE THE WORLD

Twenty nations. Seven religions. Crew and passengers. A miniature world. That is life on board the *Star Flyer* (picture), *Star Clipper* and *Royal Clipper*. The number of nations and religions may vary, but the world and the seven seas are always near. The Portuguese Nobel Prize winner José Saramago has written a beautiful little book, called *O conto da ilha desconhecida* in the original language (The Tale of the Unknown Island). A man calls on the king, demanding a ship in order to search for the unknown island. Saramago writes:

"What unknown island, asked the king, suppressing his laughter, as if he had before him one of those utter madmen obsessed with sea voyages, whom it would be as well not to cross, at least not straightaway, The unknown island, the man said again, Nonsense, there are no more unknown islands, Who told you, sir, that there are no more unknown islands, They're all on the maps, Only the known islands are on the maps, And what is this unknown island you want to go in search of, If I could tell you that, it wouldn't be unknown."

Tale of the Unknown Island is about curiosity, beauty, togetherness and love for ships and the sea. Like on the Star Clippers. Read it!

Zwanzig Nationen, sieben Religionen, Besatzung und Passagiere. Eine Welt in Miniatur. So ist das Leben an Bord der *Star Flyer*, *Star Clipper* und *Royal Clipper*. Die Anzahl der Nationen und Religionen kann sich ändern, aber die Welt und die sieben Meere sind immer gegenwärtig.

Der portugiesische Nobelpreisträger José Saramago hat ein hübsches kleines Buch geschrieben. *O conto da ilha desconhecida* (Die Geschichte von der unbekannten Insel). Ein Mann macht dem König seine Aufwartung. Er bittet um ein Schiff, um nach der unbekannten Insel zu suchen:

„Was für eine unbekannte Insel, fragte der König und unterdrückte ein Lachen, als hätte er einen völlig Verrückten vor sich, einen von denen, die sich die Seefahrt in den Kopf gesetzt haben und denen man nicht gleich zu Beginn widersprechen sollte, Die unbekannte Insel, wiederholte der Mann, Unsinn, es gibt keine unbekannten Inseln mehr, Wer hat dir denn gesagt, König, dass es keine unbekannten Inseln mehr gibt, Sie sind alle auf der Landkarte, Auf der Landkarte sind nur die bekannten Inseln, Und welche ist die unbekannte Insel, die du suchen willst, Wenn ich dir das sagen könnte, dann wäre sie nicht unbekannt, Wer hat dir denn davon erzählt, fragte der König, jetzt etwas ernster, Niemand,,

Die Geschichte von der unbekannten Insel handelt von Neugier, Schönheit, Gemeinschaft und Liebe zu Schiff und Meer.

Wie bei Star Clippers. Lesenswert!

Vingt nationalités. Sept religions. Equipage et passagers. Un monde en miniature. C'est la vie à bord du *Star Flyer*, du *Star Clipper* et du *Royal Clipper*. Le nombre de nationalités et de religions peuvent varier, mais le monde et les sept mers sont toujours présents. Le Prix Nobel portugais José Saramago a écrit un très beau petit livre, dont le titre est *O conto da ilha desconhecida* dans sa langue originale. Un homme demande au roi d'obtenir un bateau afin de trouver l'île inconnue. Saramago écrit:

« Quelle île inconnue, demanda le roi en déguisant son rire, comme s'il avait devant lui un fou délirant, un de ces fous qui ont la marotte de la navigation et qu'il ne faut surtout pas contrarier dès l'abord, L'île inconnue, répéta l'homme, Sottise, il n'y a plus d'îles inconnues, Qui t'a dit, ô roi, qu'il n'y a plus d'îles inconnues, Elles sont toutes sur les cartes, Sur les cartes il y a seulement les îles connues, Et quelle est donc cette île inconnue que tu cherches, Si je pouvais te le dire, elle ne serait plus inconnue, Qui t'en a parlé, demanda le roi, à présent plus sérieux, Personne, Dans ce cas, pourquoi t'obstines-tu à dire qu'elle existe, Simplement parce qu'il est impossible que n'existe pas une île inconnue ».

Le conte de l'île inconnue parle de la curiosité, la beauté, la solidarité et l'amour des bateaux et de la mer, comme chez Star Clippers...

Vous devriez le lire!

THE CAPTAIN and *Star Flyer crew members in Costa Rica.*

KAPITÄN *und ein Teil der Besatzung auf der Star Flyer in Costa Rica*

LE CAPITAINE *et l'équipage du Star Flyer au Costa Rica.*

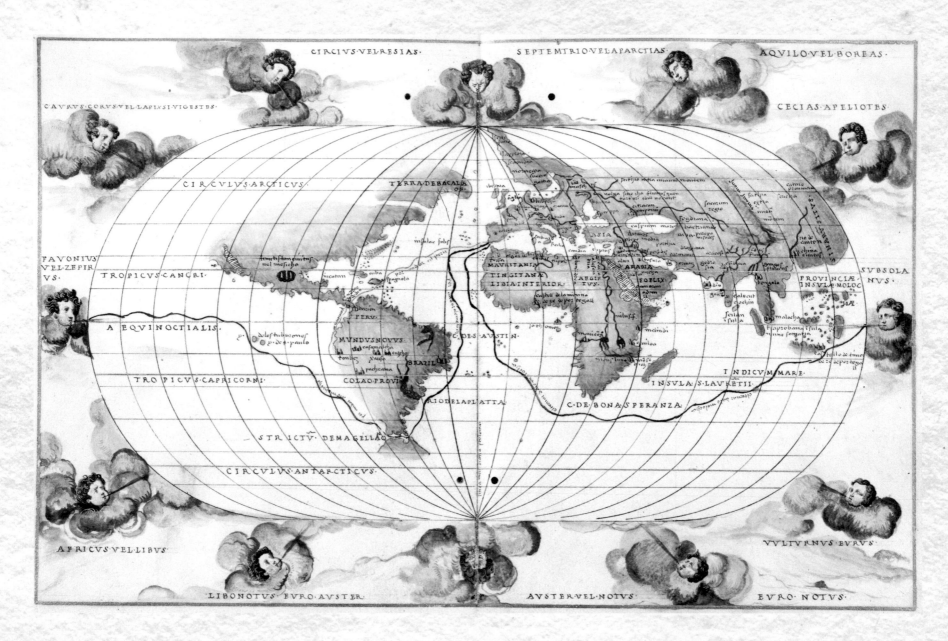

CIRCIVS·VEL·RESIAS·   SEPTEMTRIO·VEL·APARCTIAS·   AQVILO·VEL·BOREAS·

CAVRVS·CORVS·VEL·LAPIXSI·VIGESTES·   CECIAS·APELIOTES·

CIRCVLVS·ARCTICVS·   TERRA·DE·BACALAOS·

FAVONIVS VEL·ZEPIR VS·   SVBSOLA NVS·

TROPICVS·CANCRI·   MAVRITANIA   ASIA   ARABIA   PROVINCIÆ· INSVLÆ·MOLOC HIÆ

TINGITANÆ LIBIA·INTERIOR·   AEGIP TVS   FOELIX

A·EQVINOCTIALIS·   PERV   MVNDVS·NOVVS   C·DES·AVSTIN·

BRAZIL   INDICVM·MARE·

TROPICVS·CAPRICORNI·   COLAO·PROVI   INSVLA·S·LAVRETII·

RIO·DE·LA·PLATTA   C·DE·BONA·SPERANZA·

STRICTV·DE·MAGELLAO·

CIRCVLVS·ANTARCTICVS·

APRICVS·VEL·LIBVS·   VVLTVRNVS·EVRVS·

LIBONOTVS·EVRO·AVSTER·   AVSTER·VEL·NOTVS·   EVRO·NOTVS·

THE CONTINENTS look surprisingly accurate on this map by Battista Agnese from 1550.

DIE KONTINENTE sind erstaunlich richtig wiedergegeben auf dieser Karte von Batista Agnese aus dem Jahre 1550.

LES CONTINENTS semblent étonnamment précis sur la carte de Battista Agnese de 1550.

One Planet

Created to Sail

THE OCEAN UNITES. *Tall ships and small craft. Sail. Engine. Oars. Makes no difference. More than seventy per cent of the Earth's surface is water.*

DAS MEER VEREINT. *Große Schiffe und kleine Boote. Segel, Motoren, Ruder. Es spielt keine Rolle. Wasser bedeckt mehr als 70% der Erdoberfläche.*

L'OCÉAN RÉUNIT. *Grands vaisseaux et petits bateaux. A voile. A moteur. A rames. Peu importe. Plus de soixante-dix pour cent de la surface de la terre est recouverte d'eau.*

North Pacific Ocean

South Pacific Ocean

North Atlantic Ocean

Royal Clipper: Painting by Niklas Amundson ©

Indian Ocean

South Atlantic Ocean

Arctic Ocean

Southern Ocean

28

SEVEN SEAS OR NINE?

Sea of Ghee, Sea of Wine, Sea of Milk, Sea of Sugar-Cane Juice, Sea of Curds, Sea of Salt Water, Sea of Sweet Water. Seven Seas surround the sacred Mount Meru in Hindu cosmology. In Hindi, they are named Sarpi, Sura, Dughda, Ikshu, Dadhi, Lavana, and Jala.

Seven is a sacred number in most mythologies and religions. Thus, the seven seas are also found in Sumerian religion and in Greek, Roman and Christian culture.

Medieval Arabic literature lists seven seas. Their names speak of the seas familiar to Arab seafarers: Bay of Bengal, Gulf of Khambhat, Persian Gulf, Strait of Malacca, Singapore Strait, South China Sea and Gulf of Thailand.

After the great discoveries in the 16th and 17th centuries, Western tradition includes these seven seas:

The Pacific Ocean, the Atlantic Ocean, the Indian Ocean, the Arctic Ocean, the Caribbean Sea, Mediterranean Sea and the Gulf of Mexico.

In our secular age, the sacred number of seven is no longer important. There are navigators who include the Black Sea and the Caspian Sea, making the number of seas nine!

But the phrase "the Seven Seas" still sounds better than "the Nine Seas". That is probably why the British author, Nobel laureate and traveller Rudyard Kipling (1865-1936) published in 1896 a volume of poems named *The Seven Seas*.

What he esteemed was the "word music" and the "s" alliteration.

Even the scientists of today stick to the number of seven, although from a different angle. They distinguish between the bodies of water of the northern and southern hemispheres, using the word "ocean" rather than "sea". The seven oceans/seas are thus:

• North Pacific Ocean
• South Pacific Ocean
• North Atlantic Ocean
• South Atlantic Ocean
• Indian Ocean
• Southern Ocean
• Arctic Ocean.

Das Buttermeer, das Weinmeer, das Milchmeer, das Zuckermeer, das Quarkmeer, das Salzwassermeer und das Süßwassermeer. Sieben Meere umgeben den Götterberg Meru in der Hindu Mythologie. In Hindi heissen sie: Sarpi, Sura, Dugdha, Iksu, Dadhi, Lavana und Jala. Die Meere sind auch sieben an der Zahl in der Religion der Sumerer und in der griechischen, römischen und christlichen Kultur. Sogar in der arabischen Literatur des Mittelalters gibt es sieben Meere. Die Namen beschreiben die Gewässer, die den arabischen Seefahrern bekannt waren: Bucht von Bengalen, Golf von Khambhat, Straße von Malakka, Persischer Golf, Straße von Singapur, Südchinesisches Meer und Golf von Thailand.

Seit den großen Entdeckungsfahrten des sechzehnten und siebzehnten Jahrhunderts rechnet die westliche Tradition gewöhnlich mit folgenden sieben Meeren: Der Pazifische Ozean, der Indische Ozean, der Atlantische Ozean, der Arktische Ozean, das Mittelmeer, die Karibische See und der Golf von Mexiko. In unserer säkularisierten Zeit hat die heilige Zahl sieben an Bedeutung verloren. Manche Seefahrer rechnen auch das Schwarze Meer und das Kaspische Meer mit ein. Dann werden es neun Meere anstatt sieben!

Aber auf jeden Fall klingen im Englischen die Worte: „the Seven Seas" besser als „the Nine Seas." Wahrscheinlich gab der britische Verfasser, Nobelpreisträger und Weltreisende Rudyard Kipling (1865-1939) aus diesem Grunde im Jahre 1896 seine Gedichtsammlung mit dem Namen *The Seven Seas* (Die sieben Meere) heraus. Er schätzte den Klang der Worte und die Alliteration der zwei „s". Auch die Wissenschaftler der heutigen Zeit haben das Konzept der Sieben beibehalten. Sie unterscheiden zwischen den Wasserflächen auf der Nord- und der Südhalbkugel.

• Nord Pazifischer Ozean
• Süd Pazifischer Ozean
• Nord Atlantischer Ozean
• Süd Atlantischer Ozean
• Indischer Ozean
• Südlicher Ozean
• Arktischer Ozean

Mer de Beurre, Mer de Vin, Mer de Lait, Mer de Sucre de Canne, Mer de Lait Caillé, Mer d'Eau Salée, Mer d'Eau Douce. Sept Mers entourent le Mont sacré Meru en cosmologie Indienne. En langue Hindi, ils s'appellent Sarpi, Sura, Dughda, Ikshu, Dadhi, Lavana et Jala.

Le chiffre sept est un nombre sacré dans la plupart des mythologies et religions. Ainsi, les sept mers se retrouvent aussi dans la religion Sumérienne et dans les cultures Grecque, Romaine et Chrétienne.

La littérature médiévale Arabe parle aussi des sept mers. Leurs noms sont significatifs aux marins Arabes: Baie du Bengale, Golfe du Kambat, Détroit de Malacca, Golfe Persique, Détroit de Singapour, Mer du Sud de la Chine et Golfe de Thaïlande.

Après les grandes découvertes des XVI et XVII ème siècles, les traditions occidentales prennent en compte ces sept mers :

L'Océan Pacifique, l'Océan Atlantique, l'Océan Indien, l'Océan Arctique, la Mer Méditerranée, la Mer des Caraïbes et le Golfe du Mexique. Aujourd'hui le chiffre sept n'est plus aussi important. Certains navigateurs rajoutent la Mer Noire et la Mer Caspienne, ce qui fait un total de neuf mers.

Mais la phrase « les Sept Mers », en Anglais « The Seven Seas », avec l'allitération du son "s" résonne mieux que « les Neufs Mers ».

C'est probablement la raison pour laquelle l'auteur Anglais, lauréat du prix Nobel et voyageur Rudyard Kipling (1865-1936) a publié en 1896 un recueil de poèmes appelé *The Seven Seas* « Les sept Mers ».

Même les scientifiques d'aujourd'hui s'en tiennent au nombre sept. Cependant ils différencient les mers de l'hémisphère nord et celles du sud et utilisent plutôt le nom "océan". Les sept océans sont:

• Océan Pacifique Nord
• Océan Pacifique Sud
• Océan Atlantique Nord
• Océan Atlantique Sud
• Océan Indien
• Océan du Sud
• Océan Arctique.

BLOWING IN THE WIND

There are friendly, safe winds. Winds to be trusted. And there are unfriendly, dangerous and untrustworthy winds. Every sailor knows the difference. Mistral. Pampero. Williwaw. Bora. They have poetic names, but are fearsome. They may attack a ship at any time of the year and their force may suddenly go from 2 to 10 or more on the Beaufort scale.

To be suddenly hit by heavy weather is a nightmare. A storm or a hurricane can ordinarily be forecast several days ahead, but that is not the case with the Mistral and the others.

How different are the Trade Winds! The name has a lovely ring. A wind made for trade and, still better, on latitudes with a mild temperature. The north east trades give ships a following wind from Europe via Africa to the Caribbean and South America. They normally set in south of the Canary Islands. They brought Columbus across the Atlantic. These same winds give Star Clippers' tall ships a pleasant passage across the Atlantic in October-November each year.

The trade winds also give ships on the Pacific Ocean a following wind if they sail westward from the American continents. The north east trades blow north of the equator and the south east trades south of the equator.

The monsoons of the Indian Ocean are also reliable winds. Monsoon is an Arabic word, *mawsim*, meaning season. They are seasonal winds, caused by differences in temperature between the sea and the continents. The summer monsoon blows from the sea onto a warmed land, often with heavy rains. The winter monsoon is dry and blows in the opposite direction. The summer monsoon in India brings the strongest winds.

Es gibt freundliche Winde, Winde, auf die man vertrauen kann. Und es gibt unfreundliche, gefährliche und unzuverlässige Winde. Jeder Seefahrer kennt den Unterschied. Mistral. Pampero. Bora. Williwaw. Das sind poetische Namen, die aber Angst einflössen. Die Windstärke kann plötzlich von 2 Beaufort auf 10 ansteigen. Stürme und Orkane können im allgemeinen tagelang vorausgesagt werden. Das ist nicht so bei Mistral und den anderen.

Wie anders sind da doch die „tradewinds" (Handelswinde). Schon der Name hat einen freundlichen Klang. Ein Wind gemacht für den Handel, außerdem auf Breitengraden mit angenehm warmen Temperaturen. Der Nordost Passat hilft den Schiffen mit Rückenwind auf dem Wege von Europa via Afrika zur Karibik und Südamerika. Er führte Kolumbus über den Atlantik. Der gleiche Wind erlaubt den Star Clippers Tall Ships angenehmes Segeln über den Atlantik im Oktober und November eines jeden Jahres.

Passatwinde sichern auch den Schiffen im Pazifischen Ozean Rückenwind, wenn sie von den amerikanischen Kontinenten nach Westen segeln. Nördlich des Äquators weht der Nordost Passat, südlich des Äquators der Südost Passat. Der Monsun im Indischen Ozean ist ebenfalls ein verlässlicher Wind. Monsun ist ein arabisches Wort, *mawsim*, und bedeutet Jahreszeit. Es handelt sich also um jahreszeitliche Winde. Sie werden durch die Temperaturunterschiede zwischen dem Meer und den Kontinenten verursacht. Der Sommermonsun weht vom Meer zu einer aufgewärmten Landmasse hin, oft mit kräftigen Regenfällen. Der Wintermonsun ist trocken und weht in entgegengesetzter Richtung, nachdem sich die Landmasse abgekühlt hat.

Certains vents sont fiables et bienfaisants, tandis que d'autres sont traîtres et dangereux. Chaque marin connaît la différence. Mistral. Bora. Pampero. Williwaw. Bora. Ils ont des noms poétiques, mais ils sont redoutables. Ils peuvent s'attaquer à un bateau à n'importe quel moment de l'année et leur force peut monter brusquement de 2 à 10 sur l'échelle de Beaufort.

Être frappé soudainement par le mauvais temps est un cauchemar. Une tempête ou un ouragan peuvent être annoncés plusieurs jours à l'avance, mais des vents comme le Mistral, le Sirocco ou d'autres sont difficiles à prévoir.

Au contraire, le doux nom des Alizés est synonyme de conditions clémentes; en Anglais ils s'appellent Trade Winds (vents commerciaux). Les Alizés du nord offrent aux bateaux un vent favorable de l'Europe vers les Caraïbes et l'Amérique du Sud via l'Afrique. Ils ont porté Christophe Colomb à travers l'Atlantique et permettent aux voiliers Star Clippers de faire une traversée agréable en Octobre-Novembre de chaque année.

Les Alizés offrent également aux bateaux sur l'Océan Pacifique un vent favorable s'ils naviguent vers l'ouest en venant des continents américains.

Les alizés du nord-est soufflent au nord de l'équateur et les alizés du sud-est soufflent au sud de l'équateur. Les vents de la mousson sont aussi des vents sur qui on peut compter. Mousson est un mot arabe, « *mawsim* », qui signifie saison. Ce sont des vents saisonniers, engendrés par une différence de température entre la mer et les continents. En été la mousson souffle de la mer vers la côte plus chaude, souvent avec de fortes pluies. En hiver la mousson est sèche et souffle dans la direction opposée, quand la masse terrestre a refroidi.

PREVAILING winds on earth.

VORHERRSCHENDE Winde auf der Erde.

VENTS dominants sur la terre.

WIND SPEED

Strangely enough, wind speed is measured differently in different countries. Knots and Beaufort are the most common units. Anglo-Saxon countries most often use Beaufort, a scale from 1806. It was devised by Rear Admiral Sir Francis Beaufort, Royal Navy. It is not an absolute scale of wind speed, but rather a subjective description of the effects of the wind.

Originally, it described the effects of the wind on the sails of a naval ship. The scale goes from 0 to 12.

0 Beaufort is calm.
3 Beaufort is gentle breeze.
6 Beaufort is strong breeze.
8 Beaufort is gale.
12 Beaufort is hurricane.

WINDGESCHWINDIGKEIT

Erstaunlicherweise wird Windgeschwindigkeit in unterschiedlichen Ländern unterschiedlich gemessen. Beaufort und Knoten sind am gebräuchlichsten. Die angelsächsischen Länder benutzen meistens Beaufort, eine Skala aus dem Jahre 1805. Sie wurde festgelegt von Sir Francis Beaufort, Konteradmiral in der britischen Marine. Es handelt sich nicht um eine absolute Skala sondern eine mehr subjektive Beschreibung der Windeffekte. Ursprünglich ging es darum, wie der Wind auf die Segel eines Kriegsschiffes einwirkt. Die Skala reicht von 0 -12. Beaufort 0 bedeutet Flaute. 9 Beaufort Sturm. 12 Beaufort Orkan.

VITESSE DU VENT

La vitesse du vent est mesurée différemment dans différents pays. Nœuds et Beaufort sont les unités les plus communes. Les pays anglo-saxons utilisent souvent le Beaufort, une unité qui date de 1806. Elle a été inventée par le Contre-Amiral Sir Francis Beaufort de la Royal Navy. Ce n'est pas une échelle absolue de la vitesse du vent, mais plutôt une description subjective des effets du vent. L'échelle va de 0 à 12.

0 Beaufort représente une mer calme.
5 Beaufort bonne brise.
8 Beaufort vent fort.
12 Beaufort ouragan.

31

A LINE THAT DIVIDED THE WORLD

In 1494, Pope Alexander VI drew a border in mid-Atlantic. It was a line from north to south, dividing the Atlantic in two. The Treaty of Tordesillas, as it is known, deals with great power politics. It reads: "As Columbus has discovered faraway islands and lands, which have hitherto not been known, I, Alexander VI, award all these newly discovered islands and lands and all which are still to be discovered to you and your heirs and forbid all others to do trade without your permission."

He to whom the newly discovered and as yet undiscovered islands were awarded, was not Columbus, but his master, the King of Spain. To soothe the other great seafaring nation, Portugal, the Pope awarded the Portuguese monarch this sovereignty over the eastern hemisphere. That was eventually to lead to complicated relations between Portugal and Spain.

If you are familiar with the Treaty of Tordesillas, it is easy to understand why the Portuguese Vasco da Gama a few years after the signing of the treaty sailed eastward and discovered the sea route around Africa - and thus the sea route to the profitable Spice Islands in South-East Asia.

It also explains why the Spaniard Vasco Núñez de Balboa sailed westward, reached Central America and discovered the Pacific Ocean after having negotiated with great difficulty the land route across the Isthmus of Panama. That was 1513.

Consequently, the Portuguese Magellan should have sailed eastward - and so he did in his first expeditions. He sailed to India in 1505, took part in the conquest of Malacca in 1509, and salvaged two ships that were beached on the Maldives in 1510.

However, during the war years in India, he had a conflict with his superiors and returned home.

During a military campaign in Morocco, he was wounded in the leg. Crippled and misunderstood, Magellan sought a new master, and in 1517, he called on King Charles I of Spain. Magellan presented his plans to find the sea route to the Spice Islands by sailing westward - in the Spanish sphere of interest. The King listened and an agreement was drawn up, specifying among other things:

- Magellan could only sail in the Spanish half of the world - that is westward.
- He was given the sole privilege for three years to seek the sea route around America.
- One fifth of the profit of the first voyage would go to Magellan.
- If new islands were discovered, one twentieth share of the profit from them would go to Magellan.

Spain put five ships at Magellan's disposal and appointed him Captain General with power of life and death on board.

The name of the flagship was *Trinidad*. An important crew member was Antonio Pigafetta, who wrote a detailed diary.

With "frames as soft as butter" and torches burning in the stern, the ships left the port of Sanlúcar on September 20, 1519. Of the five ships and 270 men that sailed out on the first circumnavigation of the Earth, only one ship and 18 men would return, after having sailed for exactly three years. Magellan was killed in a fight on the Philippines. One of those who returned was Pigafetta. On reaching home, he asked about the day of the week and got the answer: "Thursday."

"It greatly surprised me", he writes in his diary, "as to us it was Wednesday, and I had carefully kept my diary every day."

Today we know the explanation. One day is lost if you sail westward around the Earth.

m Jahre 1494 zog der Papst Alexander VI eine Grenze mitten im Atlantik. Es war eine Linie von Nord nach Süd, die den Atlantik in der Mitte teilte. Der Vertrag von Tordesillas , wie er genannt wird, hat mit großer Politik zu tun. So steht es geschrieben: „Während Columbus fern gelegene Inseln und Länder entdeckt hat, die bisher nicht bekannt waren, geben Wir, Alexander VI, alle diese neu entdeckten Inseln und Länder und alle, die noch entdeckt werden, an Euch und Eure Erben und verbieten allen anderen, ohne Eure Zustimmung Handel zu treiben".

Jedoch nicht Kolumbus erhielt die neu entdeckten und noch nicht entdeckten Inseln, sondern sein Auftragsgeber, der spanische König.

Um die andere große seefahrende Nation - Portugal - etwas zu beruhigen, gab der Papst dem portugiesischen Regenten das Recht auf die östliche Hälfte der Welt. Wenn man den Vertrag von Tordesillas kennt, versteht man, warum der Portugiese Vasco da Gama nur ein paar Jahre nach dem Vertrag, im Jahre 1497, nach Osten segelte und den Seeweg um Afrika entdeckte - und damit den Zugang zu den gewinnbringenden Gewürzinseln in Südostasien.

Der Spanier, Vasco Nunes Balboa segelte dagegen westwärts, erreichte Mittelamerika und entdeckte den Pazifischen Ozean, nachdem er unter großen Schwierigkeiten die Landenge von Panama überwunden hatte. Das war am 25. September 1513. Der Portugiese Magellan musste also nach Osten segeln und während seiner ersten Expeditionen hielt er sich auch daran. Im Jahre 1505 segelte er nach Indien, nahm an der Eroberung Malakkas im Jahre 1509 teil und rettete 1510 zwei Schiffe, die in den Malediven gestrandet waren. Während der Kriegsjahre in Indien geriet er

EXPLORERS - CONQUERORS

Christopher Columbus
(c 1451-1506)

Vasco Balboa (c1475-1519)

Sir Francis Drake
(1540-1596)

jedoch in Schwierigkeiten mit seinen Vorgesetzten und kehrte in sein Heimatland zurück.

Im Jahre 1517 machte er König Karl V. von Spanien seine Aufwartung. Magellan präsentierte seine Pläne, den Seeweg zu den Gewürzinseln zu finden, indem er nach Westen segelte - also in der spanischen Interessensphäre. Der König hörte ihn an und man schloss einen Vertrag, der unter anderem beinhaltete:

• Magellan durfte nur in der spanischen Hälfte der Erde segeln, also westwärts.

• Für drei Jahre erhielt er allein das Recht, den Seeweg rund um Amerika zu finden.

• Ein Fünftel des Gewinns der ersten Reise sollte Magellan zufallen.

Spanien stellte Magellan fünf Schiffe zur Verfügung. Das Flaggschiff hieß *Trinidad*. Ein wichtiges Besatzungsmitglied war Antonio Pigafetta, der ein detailliertes Tagebuch schrieb. Mit brennenden Fackeln auf dem Achterdeck verließen die Schiffe die Hafenstadt San Lucar am 20. September 1519. Mit 270 Mann an Bord begann eine Fahrt, die zur ersten Umsegelung der Erde werden sollte.

Von den fünf Schiffen, die die Reise antraten, kehrte nur eins von der Erdumrundung zurück. Die Fahrt dauerte fast genau drei Jahre und von den 270 Besatzungsmitgliedern kehrten nur 18 heim. Magellan selbst wurde bei einem Kampf in den Philippinen getötet. Einer der Rückkehrer war Pigafetta. Als er bei seiner Ankunft nach dem Wochentag fragte, erhielt er die Antwort: Donnerstag. „Das verwunderte mich im höchsten Grade" schreibt er in seinem Tagebuch, „weil es für uns ein Mittwoch war und ich das Tagebuch jeden Tag sorgfältig geführt hatte." Heute kennen wir die Erklärung. Wenn man die Erde in Richtung Westen umsegelt, geht ein Tag verloren.

En 1494, le Pape Alexandre VI a tracé une frontière au milieu de l'Atlantique. C'était une ligne du nord au sud, divisant l'Atlantique en deux. Le Traité de Tordesillas, c'est ainsi qu'il est connu, était une négociation entre les grandes puissances politiques. Il y est écrit :

« Etant donné que Christophe Colomb a découvert des terres et des îles lointaines et toutes celles qui restent à découvrir par vous et vos héritiers il est interdit à tous les autres de commercer sans votre autorisation. »

Celui à qui les dernières découvertes ainsi que les îles inconnues étaient décernées n'était pas Christophe Colomb, mais son maître, le Roi d'Espagne. Afin d'apaiser l'autre grande nation maritime, le Portugal, le Pape a autorisé la souveraineté de la monarchie portugaise sur l'hémisphère est.

Si vous connaissez bien le Traité de Tordesillas, il est facile de comprendre que le portugais Vasco de Gama quelques années après la signature du traité, a navigué vers l'est et a découvert la route maritime autour de l'Afrique - et ainsi la route maritime vers les épices lucratives des îles du sud-est asiatique. De la même manière l'espagnol Vasco Nunez de Balboa a navigué vers l'ouest, atteignant l'Amérique Centrale où il a découvert l'Océan Pacifique après avoir négocié avec grande difficulté le passage par la terre à travers l'isthme de Panama. C'était en 1513.

Le portugais Magellan, lui, avait dû naviguer vers l'est - ce qu'il fit pendant ses premières expéditions. Il a atteint l'Inde en 1505 et prit part à la conquête de Malacca en 1509.

Toutefois, pendant les années de guerre en Inde, il eut un conflit avec ses supérieurs et rentra au Portugal. Estropié et incompris, Magellan recherchait un nouveau voilier, et en 1517, il s'adressa au roi Charles I d'Espagne. Magellan présenta ses plans pour trouver la route vers les îles aux épices en naviguant vers l'ouest à travers le territoire réservé aux intérêts espagnols. Le roi l'écouta et lui donna son accord, selon les termes suivants :

• Magellan pouvait naviguer seulement dans la moitié espagnole du monde c'est-à-dire vers l'ouest.

• Pendant trois ans, il lui était donné le privilège unique de rechercher la route maritime autour de l'Amérique.

• Un cinquième des profits du premier voyage serait pour lui.

L'Espagne mit cinq vaisseaux à la disposition de Magellan et le nomma Capitaine général avec le pouvoir de vie et de mort à bord.

Le nom de la flotte était Trinidad. Un membre important de l'équipage, Antonio Pigafetta, écrivait le journal de bord.

Avec « des règles aussi douces que du beurre » et des torches brûlant à l'arrière, les bateaux quittèrent le port de Sanlucar le 20 septembre 1519. Sur les cinq navires et 270 hommes, qui ont fait pour la première fois le tour de la terre, seul un bateau et 18 hommes sont rentrés, après avoir navigué exactement pendant trois ans. Magellan fut tué pendant un combat aux Philippines. Parmi ceux qui sont rentrés, il y avait Pigafetta. Rentrant au pays, il a demandé quel était le jour de la semaine et il obtint la réponse : « Jeudi. »

« Cela m'étonne beaucoup », écrit-il, « pour nous, nous étions Mercredi, et je tenais scrupuleusement mon journal de bord. »

Aujourd'hui, nous en connaissons la raison. Un jour est perdu si vous naviguez vers l'ouest autour de la terre.

Ferdinand Magellan
(c1480-1521)

Louis Bougainville
(1729-1811)

Vasco da Gama
(c1460-1524)

1992 STAR CLIPPER

Type of vessel	Barquentine	Number of sails	16
Hull material	Steel	Sail area	3,365 sq m (36,173 sq ft)
Length	115,5 m (379 ft)	Mast height	63 m (207 ft)
Beam	15 m (49 ft)	Crew	74
Draught	5,6 m (18 ft)	Passengers	170
Displacement	2 298 tons	Time to cross Atlantic	14 days
Number of masts	4	Average speed	9 knots

Type of vessel	Carrack (?)	**Number of sails**	15
Hull material	Wood	**Sail area**	330 sq m (3500 sq ft)
Length	24 m (80 ft)	**Crew**	40
Beam	8 m (26 ft)	**Captain**	Christopher Columbus
Draught	2 m (7 ft)	**Time to cross Atlantic**	37 days
Displacement	100 tons	**Average speed**	4 knots
Number of masts	3		

FEAR OF LAND

Seamen avoid land. Not brawls in disreputable bars, but rocky coasts and shallow shores with tidal currents. As a matter of fact, marine disasters rarely occur in storms at sea. It is much more dangerous to be sailing along a coast, and worst of all is when the wind blows towards the land. A lee shore is dangerous - even today.

On March 16, 1978, the VLCC (Very Large Crude Oil Carrier) *Amoco Cadiz* had a steering mechanism failure off Brittany in France. In a strong wind, she drifted onto the rocks and more than 200,000 tons of oil spilled out.

In the age of sail, the dangers were still greater. Charts and navigational aids were unreliable. The ships' capacity to beat away from a leeward shore was limited. Emergency anchoring was the only chance of saving ship, crew and cargo. If the anchor did not hold, the ship was doomed. There are famous ships' graveyards off the coasts of Maine in the USA, Galicia in Spain, Brittany, France and the Orkney and Shetland Islands.

The waters around the Isles of Scilly and Penzance at the western entrance to the English Channel are both infamous and well documented. For five generations, the Gibson family of the Scillies has specialised in photographing shipwrecks - as in this picture from 1888.

IN 1888, the Jeune Hortense is wrecked near Penzance. Spectators, life-savers and photographer Herbert Gibson are there.

DAS JAHR 1888, Jeune Hortense ist bei Penzance auf Grund gelaufen. Schaulustige, Seenotretter und Fotograf Herbert Gibson sind zur Stelle.

EN 1888, la Jeune Hortense fait naufrage près de Penzance. Des spectateurs, des sauveteurs et le photographe Herbert Gibson sont présents.

Seeleute meiden das Land; nicht wegen Schlägereien in Hafenkneipen, sondern wegen felsiger Meeresküsten und seichten Stränden mit Gezeitenströmungen. Tatsächlich kommen Seeunglücke selten im Sturm auf offenem Meer vor. Weit gefährlicher ist es, entlang einer Küste zu segeln und am ärgsten ist es, wenn der Wind zur Küste hin weht. Land zu Lee ist gefährlich - auch heute noch. Wie 16. März 1978. Da fiel bei der *Amoco Cadiz*, (ein großer Öltanker) die Steueranlage aus, als sich das Schiff vor der Bretagne in Frankreich befand. In einem harten auflandigen Wind trieb sie auf Grund. Über 200 000 Tonnen Öl liefen aus.

In der Zeit der Segelschiffe waren die Gefahren noch größer. Seekarten und Navigationshilfen waren unzuverlässig und vor allem war es für die Schiffe schwierig, von der Küste wegzusegeln, wenn der Wind landeinwärts blies. Notankern war die einzige Möglichkeit, Schiff, Besatzung und Fracht zu retten. Hielt der Anker nicht, war das Schiff verloren.

Bekannte Schiffsfriedhöfe befinden sich an den Küsten von Main, USA, Galizien, Spanien, Bretagne, Frankreich und bei den Orkney - und Shetland-inseln. Die Gewässer um die Scilly Inseln und die Stadt Penzance an dem schmalen westlichen Eingang zum Ärmelkanal sind ebenfalls berüchtigt und außerdem gut dokumentiert. Die Familie Gibson auf Scilly hat sich über fünf Generationen darauf spezialisiert, Schiffbrüche zu fotografieren -wie dieses Bild von 1888.

Les marins évitent la terre. Non pas par risque de bagarre dans des bars de mauvaise réputation, mais surtout à cause des côtes rocheuses, des fonds peu profonds et des courants de marée. En fait, les désastres maritimes arrivent rarement en mer pendant les tempêtes. Il est beaucoup plus dangereux de naviguer près des côtes, surtout lorsque le vent souffle vers la côte. Une côte sous le vent est dangereuse - même de nos jours.

En 1978, un gros pétrolier, l'*Amoco Cadiz* eut une panne mécanique au niveau du gouvernail au large de la Bretagne en France. Par vent fort, il fût entraîné sur les rochers. Le bateau s'est cassé et cela a été l'un des désastres pétroliers les plus importants au monde. Plus de 200 000 tonnes de pétrole se sont écoulées.

A l'époque de la navigation à voile, les dangers s'avéraient encore plus grands. Les cartes et les aides à la navigation étaient peu fiables. Jeter l'ancre constituait la seule chance de sauver le bateau, l'équipage et la cargaison. Si l'ancre n'accrochait pas, le bateau était condamné. Il existe de nombreux cimetières de bateaux le long de la côte du Maine aux USA, en Galicie en Espagne, en Bretagne en France, aux Orkney, et aux îles Schetland.

Les eaux autour des Iles Scilly et de Penzance à l'entrée ouest de la Manche sont toutes les deux mal réputées. Pendant cinq générations, la famille Gibson des Iles Scilly était spécialisée dans les reportages photographiques des naufrages.

Ainsi en témoigne cette photo de 1888.

CAPE HORN WORST OF ALL

When the four-mast barque *C B Pedersen* rounded Cape Horn in 1929, the Southern Ocean was almost like a mirror (picture). The captain had dared to sail close to the most notorious rock in the world. So, sometimes even Cape Horn weather can be calm. A seaman wrote: "We hadn't had any altitude in the sun, so we were happy when we caught a glimpse of the familiar silhouette of Cape Horn between the blizzards. The weather was fairly good, so even our little black pigs August and Petter could take a walk under the fo'c'sle deck, while we cleaned the sty."

But such weather is exceptional. At Cape Horn, there is a westerly gale or storm one day out of three. It rains or snows 360 days a year.

Cape Horn is situated on latitude 55°59' South. The fiftieth latitudes are infamous, sailors call them The Screaming Fifties. The low pressures that form over Antarctica can chase around the world without any obstacles. There are no great land masses in their way. Wind and waves are worse than anywhere else on Earth. The ships that sailed from Australia to Europe took advantage of the westerly winds, rounding Cape Horn from west to east with a following wind. It was tougher for those who sailed in the opposite direction, ships bound from the US east coast to the west coast or sailing from Europe to fetch cargoes of nitrate, guano or copper in Chile and Peru.

For weeks or even months, they would struggle against heavy head winds to round Cape Horn. Clouds, poor visibility and rain made navigation uncertain. Weeks might pass before captain and officers had a chance to see sun, moon and stars and have a reliable sextant observation.

AN EXCLUSIVE CLUB

Cape Horn W.by S.

Those who had rounded Cape Horn in a commercial sailing vessel without an auxiliary engine could in former times join one of the world's most exclusive clubs: The "Amicale Internationale des Capitaines au Long-Cours Cap Horniers" (A.I.C.H.) in St. Malo, Brittany. At one time, it had more than 2,000 members.

But there are no longer any sailing ships without an engine, and the last rounding of Cape Horn in such a ship took place more than sixty years ago. Today, it is doubtful whether any genuine Cape Horner is still alive. The Society was dissolved in 2003.

Cape Horn was first sighted in 1615. It was by two ships from the little Dutch town of Hoorn. Their names were *Eendracht* and *Hoorn*, commanded by Willem Schouten. He was searching for a southern route around South America, by which he would reach the Spice Islands near New Guinea. But why did he not sail through the Strait of Magellan, discovered almost a hundred years earlier? Shipping was strictly regulated even then. Only ships belonging to the powerful Dutch East India Company were allowed to use the Strait.

It was commonly held at this time that the Strait of Magellan was the only passage between the Atlantic and the Pacific Ocean. Tierra del Fuego, south of the Strait, was believed to be the beginning of a continent, stretching past the South Pole. However, Schouten thought, there might be another route further south.

So, the *Eendracht* and the *Hoorn* sailed past the entrance to the Strait and continued southwards along the Tierra del Fuego. At eight in the evening on January 29, Schouten discovered a headland. He is said to have shouted "Kaap Hoorn! Kaap Hoorn!" and thus named the headland, which is actually an island, after his home town.

Schouten had already named Staten Island, east of Tierra del Fuego after his home country (the Estates-General) and Le Maire Strait after his financier. From Cape Horn, Schouten proceeded to the Spice Islands. There, he was immediately arrested and charged with having sailed through the Strait of Magellan. He was brought to Holland as a prisoner, but by showing his logbooks he was acquitted and the East India Company had to compensate him for his loss of ships, cargo and equipment.

Als der Viermaster *C B Pedersen* das Kap Horn 1929 umrundete, war der südliche Ozean fast spiegelglatt (Bild). Der Kapitän wagte sich nah an die Klippe mit dem gefürchtesten Ruf der Welt heran. So ist das, manchmal ist es auch am Kap Horn ruhig. Ein Seemann schrieb: „Die Sonnenhöhe konnten wir nicht feststellen daher waren wir froh, als wir zwischen heftigen Schnee-schauern die wohlbekannte Silhouette von Kap Horn sichteten. Wir hatten relativ schönes Wetter, so dass sogar unsere zwei schwarzen Schweine, August und Petter, sich eine Promenade unter dem Vorderdeck leisten konnten, während wir den Stall ausmisteten."

Aber ein solches Wetter gehört zu den Aus-nahmen. Am Kap Horn bläst ein westlicher starker Wind oder Sturm an mindestens einem von drei Tagen. Es regnet oder schneit an 360 Tagen im Jahr. Kap Horn liegt auf 55°59' S. Die fünfzigsten Breitengrade sind berüchtigt. The Screaming Fifties (die heulenden Funfziger) heißen sie in der Seemannssprache. Die Tiefdruckgebiete, die sich über der Antarktis bilden, können ungestört um die Welt eilen. Die Westwinde wurden von den Schiffen ausgenutzt, die von Australien nach Europa segelten. Sie umrundeten Kap Horn mit Rückenwind von Westen nach Osten. Schwieriger war es, in der Gegenrichtung zu segeln, also für Schiffe, die von der Ostküste der USA zur West-küste oder von Europa nach Chile und Peru fuhren, um Salpeter, Guano und Kupfer zu laden.

Für Wochen, manchmal Monate, mussten sie gegen heftige Winde kämpfen, um Kap Horn zu umrunden. Kap Horn wurde zum ersten Mal 1615 gesichtet. Es waren zwei Schiffe der holländischen Kleinstadt Hoorn. Sie hießen *Eendracht* und *Hoorn*

EXKLUSIVER KLUB

Wer Kap Horn in einem segelnden Handelsschiff ohne Hilfsmotor umrundet hatte, konnte früher Mitglied in einer der exklusivsten Vereinigungen der Welt werden: Amicale Internationale des Capitainesau Long-Cors, Cap-Horniers (A.I.C.H.) Die Gesellschaft wurde 1937 in Saint Malo in der Bretagne gegründet. Sie hatte einmal über 2000 Mitglieder. Aber segelnde Handelsschiffe ohne Motor gibt es heute nicht mehr und die letzte Kap Horn Umrundung mit einem der-artigen Schiff fand vor mehr als 60 Jahren statt. Heute ist es zweifelhaft, ob noch ein echter Kap Horner am Leben ist. Der Verein wurde 2003 geschlossen.

UN CLUB EXCLUSIF TRES FERME

Ceux qui ont franchi le Cap Horn sur un voilier de commerce sans moteur pouvaient entrer dans l'un de ces clubs les plus fermés du monde: l' Amicale Internationale des Capitaines au Long-Cours Cap Horniers (A.I.C.H.) à Saint Malo en Bretagne. Il y avait plus de 2 000 membres. Mais il n'y a plus aucun voilier sans moteur, et le dernier franchissement du Cap Horn avec un tel navire s'est produit il y a plus de soixante ans. Aujourd'hui, il est incertain qu'il y ait encore de véritable Cap Hornier encore vivant. Le club fut dissout en 2003.

und standen unter dem Kommando von Willem Schouten. Er suchte einen südlichen Weg von Südamerika zu den Gewürzinseln nahe Neuguinea. Aber warum segelte er nicht durch die Magellanstraße, die beinahe hundert Jahre früher entdeckt worden war? Die Seefahrt war schon damals streng reguliert. Die Magellanstraße durften nur Schiffe passieren, die der mächtigen niederländischen Ostindien-Compagnie angehörten. Schouten und sein Gönner Isaac Le Maire waren keine Mitglieder der Compagnie.

Nach allgemeiner Ansicht jener Zeit war die Magellanstraße die einzige Verbindung zwischen Atlantik und Pazifik. Man glaubte, dass Feuerland, südlich der Straße, der Anfang eines Kontinents war, der sich über den Südpol hinaus erstreckte. Aber Schouten dachte, es gäbe vielleicht einen südlicheren Weg. Die Schiffe *Eendracht* und *Hoorn* segelten also am Eingang zur Magellanstraße vorbei und fuhren weiter in Richtung Süden entlang der Küste von Feuerland.

Um acht Uhr abends am 29. Januar entdeckte Schouten eine Landzunge: „Kap Hoorn! Kap Hoorn!" soll er gerufen haben und benannte damit die Klippe, die eigentlich eine Insel ist, nach seiner Heimatstadt. Schouten hatte bereits Staten Island, östlich von Feuerland, nach seinem Heimatland und die Le Maire Strait nach seinem Gönner benannt.

Von Kap Horn segelte Schouten weiter zu den Gewürzinseln. Dort wurde er prompt verhaftet und angeklagt, die Magellanstraße passiert zu haben. Er wurde als Gefangener nach Holland gebracht, wurde aber aufgrund seiner Logbücher freigesprochen und die Ostindien-Compagnie musste den Verlust von Schiff, Ladung und Ausrüstung ersetzen.

L orsque la barque quatre mâts *C B Pedersen* passa le Cap Horn en 1929, l'Océan du Sud était comme un miroir. Le capitaine osa naviguer près du rocher le plus mal réputé du monde. Mais même au Cap Horn, les conditions météorologiques pouvaient être parfois calmes. Un marin a écrit: « Nous n'avions pas vu le soleil après des jours de tempêtes et étions très heureux d'apercevoir la silhouette familière du Cap Horn entre les grains. Le temps était assez beau, et même nos petits cochons noirs August et Petter ont pu faire une marche sur le pont supérieur, pendant que nous nettoyions la porcherie. »

Mais un tel temps est exceptionnel. Au Cap Horn, il y a des coups de vent ou une tempête un jour sur trois. Il pleut ou il neige 360 jours par an. Le Cap Horn se situe au 55°59' sud. Les latitudes autour des cinquantièmes sont terribles, les marins les appellent les Cinquantièmes Rugissants. Les basses pressions qui se forment au dessus de l'Antartique peuvent parcourir le monde sans aucun obstacle. Il n'y a pas de grandes masses terrestres dans cette région. Le vent et les vagues sont plus gros ici que n'importe où sur la terre.

Les bateaux qui naviguent depuis l'Australie pour l'Europe ont l'avantage de bénéficier des vents d'ouest portants, qui passent le Cap Horn d'ouest en est. C'était terrible pour ceux qui naviguaient dans la direction opposée, tels les bateaux en partance de la côte est des Etats-Unis pour la côte ouest, ou ceux qui venaient d'Europe pour charger des cargaisons de nitrate, de guano ou du cuivre du Chili et du Pérou. Pendant des semaines et même des mois, ils devaient lutter contre des vents forts de face pour passer le Cap Horn. C'est en 1615 que le Cap Horn a été

franchi pour la première fois, par deux bateaux d'une petite ville hollandaise du nom de Hoorn. Ils s'appelaient le *Eendracht* et le *Hoorn*, commandés par Willem Schouten. Ils recherchaient une route sud autour de l'Amérique du Sud, par laquelle ils auraient pu atteindre les îles aux épices près de la Nouvelle Guinée. Mais pourquoi ne sont-ils pas passés par le Détroit de Magellan, découvert presque cent ans plus tôt? Les affrètements étaient déjà strictement régulés. Seuls les vaisseaux appartenant à la puissante Société Hollandaise de l'Inde de l'Est étaient autorisés à utiliser le Détroit. Il était communément reconnu en ce temps là que le Détroit de Magellan était le seul passage entre l'Atlantique et l'Océan Pacifique. La Tierra del Fuego, au sud du Détroit, était reconnue comme étant le début d'un continent s'étendant au delà du Pôle Sud. Mais, Schouten pensait qu'il pouvait y avoir une autre route plus au sud.

C'est ainsi que le *Eendracht* et le *Hoorn* naviguèrent en passant le Détroit et continuèrent au sud le long de la Tierra del Fuego. Le soir du 29 janvier, Schouten découvrit un cap à l'avant et se mit à crier « Kaap Hoorn! Kaap Hoorn! » Ainsi se nomma ce cap, qui est en fait une île, comme sa destination. Schouten avait déjà dénommé l'Ile de Staten, à l'est de la Tierra del Fuego, qui porte le nom de sa ville et de Le Maire, qui était le nom de son investisseur.

Depuis le Cap Horn, Schouten se dirigea vers les îles aux épices. Là, il fût immédiatement arrêté et embarqué pour avoir navigué à travers le Détroit de Magellan. Il fut emmené en Hollande comme un prisonnier, mais grâce à son carnet de bord il fut acquitté et la Société de l'Est de l'Inde a dû le dédommager pour la perte de ses bateaux, cargaison et équipements.

RUBBER INFLATABLE TO CAPE HORN

In 1987 Erling Matz, the author of this book, reached Cape Horn in a 4.5 metre (15 ft) inflatable rubber boat. With him was his wife Carina. "I had just written a book about the passages of the great sailing vessels around Cape Horn. The book also tells about the Indians who lived in this inhospitable area until 100 years ago. They paddled between the islands in primitive canoes. I thought that in that case, it should be possible to do the same thing in a rubber boat. The voyage took two weeks, starting in Ushuaia, which claims to be the southernmost city in the world."

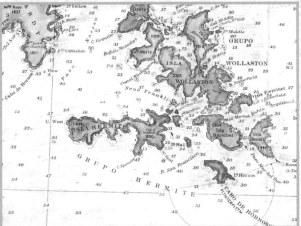

CHART. *The islands round Cape Horn.*
- The church spire in the town of Hoorn and the harbour tower were already in existence when Schouten departed from here in the early 17th century.
- But today, the harbour is full of pleasure craft.

SEEKARTE. *Die Inseln um Kap Horn.*
- Den Kirchturm und den Hafenturm in der Stadt Hoorn gab es bereits als Schouten hier Anfang des 17. Jahrhunderts seine Fahrt begann.
- Heute ist der Hafen voll von Freizeitbooten.

CARTE. *Les îles autour du Cap Horn.*
- La flèche de l'église de la ville de Hoorn et la tour du port, déjà présente lorsque Schouten est parti au début du XVII ème siècle.
- Désormais, le port est rempli de bateaux de plaisance.

IM GUMMIBOOT NACH KAP HORN

Erling Matz, der Verfasser dieses Buches, fuhr 1987 zusammen mit seiner Frau Carina in einem 4,5 m langen Gummiboot zum Kap Horn. „Ich hatte gerade ein Buch über die Umsegelung Kap Horns durch die großen Schiffe geschrieben. Aber das Buch handelte auch von den Indianern, die bis vor hundert Jahren in diesen unwirtlichen Gefilden lebten. Sie paddelten zwischen den Inseln in Kanus. Ich dachte, dass es dann möglich sein sollte dasselbe auch mit einem Gummiboot zu tun. Die Fahrt von Ushuaia, der südlichsten Stadt der Welt, dauerte zwei Wochen."

UN PNEUMATIQUE INSUBMERSIBLE POUR LE CAP HORN

Erling Matz, l'auteur de ce livre a atteint en 1987 le Cap Horn sur un pneumatique insubmersible de 4,5 m. Sa femme Carina l'accompagnait. Il a écrit un livre à propos des passages du Cap Horn par les grands voiliers. Mais l'ouvrage décrit aussi les Indiens qui vivaient dans cette région inhospitalière jusqu'à il y a une centaine d'années. Ils pagayaient entre les îles sur des canoés. Compte tenu de cela, je pensais possible de faire de même sur un pneumatique. Le voyage m'a pris deux semaines, partant d'Ushuaia, la ville la plus au sud du monde.

Faster
Speed Means Money

THE LAST VOYAGES. There were freights where speed and time meant everything. First to port meant greater profit. The cargo was tea and people.

DIE LETZTEN REISEN. Bei manchen Ladungen bedeuteten Geschwindigkeit und Zeit alles. Als Erste den Hafen zu erreichen, bedeutete einen höheren Gewinn. Die entsprechenden Ladungen waren Tee und Menschen.

LES DERNIERS VOYAGES. Il y a des chargements pour lesquels la vitesse et le temps sont très importants. Le premier arrivé au port va faire les plus grands profits. Les marchandises en question étaient le thé et les passagers.

OPIUM, PEOPLE AND TEA

The early history of the clippers is a bloody one. The fastest, most graceful ships that ever sailed the oceans were conceived by smugglers and pirates. Not so strange. Speed and agility always put you at an advantage, whether in the street or at sea. The origin of the word "clipper" is uncertain. It has been explained in several ways. One relates to the English word "clip", meaning "to run or fly swiftly" - just like the clippers. Another explanation is linked to the stem of the ship, which is designed "to clip over the waves rather than plough through them".

Thus a clipper is not one particular type of vessel. It is fast, easy to handle and built for maximum speed rather than for maximum cargo capacity. A clipper may be rigged with two or more masts; it may be a small schooner or a fully rigged ship with twenty square sails. A brig or a jackass barque.

The names of the most famous clippers were most revealing: *Lightning, Flying Cloud, Ariel, White Squall, Stag Hound, Tornado, Sea Witch ...*

The great age of the clipper ships was short, only some twenty years. It started in the late 1840's and continued until the early 1870's. During these two decades, the clippers raced across the oceans. The most important trade routes were:

1. New York - San Francisco via Cape Horn. On board were hopeful gold-diggers en route for the California gold fields. 2. China - England with tea cargoes. The captain and crew of the season's first ship in London could cash in on an extra reward. 3. India - China with opium. The opium was smuggled into China and illegally exchanged for silver, the only product the Chinese would accept in exchange for tea.

But it all started half a century earlier. The first

OPIUM smokers. 19th century. The clipper Stag Hound, 1850. Painting by Carl Hendel Friberg. (p 42)

OPIUMRAUCHER. 19. Jahrhunderts. Der Klipper Stag Hound im Jahre 1850. Gemälde von Carl Hendel Friberg. (s 42)

FUMEURS d'opium. 19è siècle. Le clipper Stag Hound, en 1850. Peinture de Carl Hendel Friberg. (p 42)

OPIUM CLIPPER

The *Wild Dayrell* was one of the British ships carrying opium to China from India. She was launched in 1855, two years before the second Opium War between Britain/France and China. Opium (although illegal) and silver were the only payment that the Chinese merchants accepted for tea, porcelain and silk. But the Chinese authorities tried to stop this widespread trade, which could reach 2,500 tons annually. The merchandise was carried in small, fast clippers, armed with cannon for protection against Chinese pirates.

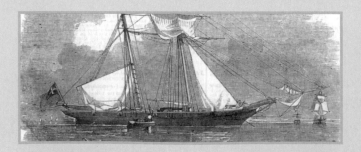

ships that we could call clippers were built in Brittany and Normandy in France around 1800. The name "clipper" did not yet exist, but the ships had similar qualities and hull shapes, which would later be widely known as cod head and mackerel tail.

The French ships were used for smuggling and privateering during the troubled Napoleonic period. Large and heavily armed British ships were an easy prey for the greyhounds of the oceans. David against Goliath. Lord Nelson reluctantly admitted that the most successful frigates of the British navy during the war against Napoleon were those captured from the French, that is, ships designed and built in France!

The heavy British ships-of-the-line had problems in the 1812 war against the United States as well. On the American east coast, a type of ship, called Baltimore Clippers, was built. They were good sailers, lightly armed and perfect for privateering. The Baltimore Clippers were very successful against the British in naval engagements on the Great Lakes and the Saint Lawrence river. A few decades later, in 1837, the British Parliament had a discussion on seamanship:

"The American ships frequenting the ports of England are stated by several witnesses to be superior to those of a similar class amongst the ships of Great Britain, the commanders and officers being generally considered to be more competent as seamen and navigators, and more uniformly persons of education, than the commanders and officers of British ships".

The American ships that so impressed the British MPs were those that sailed on scheduled runs between England and the USA. They were called packet ships. Their most frequented ports were Liverpool and New York, but they also sailed between other American and British ports and to Australia. They carried passengers, often emigrants, but also cargo.

But the American-British competition for building the fastest ships would get more intense. In 1845, Donald McKay, an inventive young shipbuilder, started designing and constructing ships at a Boston shipyard. That was the start of the brief golden age of the clippers. The American maritime historian Arthur H Clark in his great work The Clipper Ship Era (1910) states with a trace of malicious delight:

"Farewell, then, to the gallant old Indiaman, with her hammock nettings, bunt jiggers, rolling tackles, jeers, gammon lashings, bentinck shrouds, and cat harpings, dear to sailors' hearts; and goodbye to her sailors, too, sons of the men who fought in the victorious fleets of Nelson, fellows who drank gunpowder in their rum before stripping to battle with the enemy, who could stand triced up by the thumbs and take their four-and-twenty of rawhide on the naked back without wetting an eyelash. And farewell to the merry dance and song, the extra dram of grog in the dogwatch, and jovial toasts to sweethearts and wives".

Die Klipperschiffe haben eine blutige Vorgeschichte. Die schönsten, schnellsten und elegantesten Schiffe wurden von Schmugglern und Piraten entwickelt. Eigentlich nicht überraschend. Geschwindigkeit und Flexibilität sind bei allen Auseinandersetzungen ein Vorteil, egal ob sie sich auf der Straße oder auf dem Meer abspielen. Es ist nicht sicher, woher das Wort Klipperschiff kommt. Es gibt mehrere Erklärungsversuche. Einer geht zurück auf das englische Wort - clip -.

OPIUM KLIPPER

Wild Dayrell war eines der britischen Schiffe, das mit Opium von Indien nach China segelte. Sie lief 1855 vom Stapel. Die chinesischen Händler nahmen nur Opium und Silber als Bezahlung für Tee, Porzellan und Seide. Die chinesischen Behörden versuchten allerdings diesen umfangreichen Handel zu verhindern, der bis zu 2,5 Millionen Tonnen pro Jahr betragen konnte. Der Handel wurde mit gut segelnden kleinen Klipperschiffen betrieben, die zum Schutz vor chinesischen Piraten mit Kanonen bestückt waren.

LE CLIPPER A OPIUM

Le *Wild Dayrell* inauguré en 1855 était l'un des bateaux britanniques qui transportait de l'opium de l'Inde à la Chine. L'Opium (bien qu'illégal) et l'argent étaient les seuls moyens de paiement que les marchands chinois acceptaient pour le thé, la porcelaine et la soie. Mais les autorités chinoises ont essayé d'arrêter ce commerce étendu, qui pouvait atteindre annuellement 2 500 tonnes. La marchandise était transportée par des clippers légers et rapides, armés de canons pour se protéger contre les pirates chinois.

TEA is packed by treading. Chinese painting, 18th century.

TEE wird mit den Füssen verpackt. Chinesisches Gemälde aus dem 1. Jahrhundert.

THÉ tassé au pied. Peinture chinoise, 18è siècle.

Es bedeutet - laufen oder geschwind fliegen - also genau wie die Klipperschiffe. Eine andere Erklärung zielt auf das Vorschiff hin, das durch die Wellen schneidet (*Englisch clips*) und nicht durch sie pflügt. Ein Klipper ist also kein besonderer Schiffstyp sondern ein schnelles Schiff, leicht manövrierbar und für Höchstgeschwindigkeit gebaut, nicht für maximale Beladung. Ein Klipper kann zwei oder mehr Masten haben. Es kann ein kleiner Schoner mit zwei Gaffelsegeln sein oder ein Vollschiff mit zwanzig Rahsegeln, eine Brigg ....

Die Namen der berühmtesten Klipperschiffe machten deutlich, worum es ging: *Flying Cloud, Ariel, White Squall, Stag Hound, Tornado, Seawitch...*

Die Blütezeit der Klipper war kurz, gerade mal zwanzig Jahre. Sie begann zwischen 1840 und 1850 und endete um 1870. Während dieser zwei Jahrzehnte flogen die Klipperschiffe über die Meere. Die drei wichtigsten Handelsrouten waren:

1. New York - San Francisco via Kap Horn. An Bord waren die Glücksucher auf dem Weg zum Gold in Kalifornien. 2. China - England mit Ladungen von Tee. Kapitän und Besatzung des schnellsten Schiffes erhielten eine Extrabelohnung. 3. Indien - China mit Opium und Silber als Ladung. Die Chinesen akzeptierten keine andere Ware im Tausch gegen Tee.

Aber die Geschichte beginnt schon ein halbes Jahrhundert früher. Die ersten Schiffe, die man als Klipper bezeichnen kann, wurden schon zur Jahrhundertwende 1800 in Frankreich in der Bretagne und der Normandie gebaut. Den Namen Klipper gab es noch nicht, aber es waren Schiffe mit ähnlichen Eigenschaften und Schiffsformen. Letztere wurden später allgemein als Kabeljaukopf und Makrelenschwanz (Cod Head and Mackerel Tail) bezeichnet.

Während der unruhigen Zeiten unter Napoleon dienten die französischen Schiffe zum Schmuggeln und Kapern. Große und schwer bestückte englische Schiffe wurden zur leichten Beute für diese Windhunde der Meere. Admiral Nelson musste widerwillig zugeben, dass die erfolgreichsten britischen Fregatten im Kampf gegen Napoleon von den Franzosen erbeutet worden waren, also Schiffe die in Frankreich entworfen und gebaut worden. Auch im Krieg zwischen England und den USA im Jahre 1812, hatten die schweren englischen Linienschiffe Probleme. An der amerikanischen Ostküste wurde ein Schiffstyp gebaut, der den Namen Baltimore Clipper erhielt. Es war ein gut zu segelndes Schiff, leicht bestückt und hervorragend zum Kapern geeignet. Die Baltimore Clippers waren sehr erfolgreich bei den Seeschlachten mit den Engländern auf den Großen Seen und im St. Lawrence Strom.

Ein paar Jahrzehnte später, im Jahre 1837, diskutierte das Britische Parlament seemännisches Können: „Es gibt mehrere Zeugen, die behaupten, dass die amerikanischen Schiffe, die die englischen Häfen anlaufen, den vergleichbaren englischen Schiffen überlegen sind.

Die Kapitäne und Offiziere gelten allgemein als bessere Seeleute und Navigatoren und auch besser ausgebildet als die Kapitäne und Offiziere auf den englischen Schiffen".

Die britischen Parlamentsabgeordneten waren besonders von den amerikanischen Schiffen beeindruckt, die nach einem Fahrplan zwischen England und den USA segelten. Man nannte sie „Packet Ships" und ihre wichtigsten Häfen waren Liverpool und New York.

Aber die Konkurrenz zwischen den USA und England, wer die schnellsten Schiffe baute, sollte

sich noch verschärfen. Im Jahre 1845 begann Donald McKay, ein ideenreicher junger Schiffsbauer, auf einer Werft in Boston Schiffe zu konstruieren und zu bauen. Das war die Einleitung zu der kurzen Großzeit der Klipperschiffe. Der amerikanische Marinehistoriker Arthur H Clark schrieb nicht ohne Schadenfreude in seinem großen Werk von 1910 „The Clipper Ship Era": „Ein Lebewohl, denn, dem galanten alten Indienfahrer, mit seinen Hängematten, Wanten, Padune und Stagen, so nahe dem Herzen der Seemänner, und ein auf Wiedersehen für ihre Matrosen, Söhne von Männern, die in Nelsons siegreichen Flotten kämpften, Gesellen, die Schießpulver in ihrem Rum tranken, bevor sie sich klarmachten zum Gefecht mit dem Feind, die es ertragen konnten, an ihren Daumen aufgehängt ihre vierundzwanzig Peitschenschläge auf den blanken Rücken zu ertragen, ohne eine Träne im Auge zu zeigen."

Le début de l'histoire des clippers est tâché de sang. Les plus rapides, les plus élégants et harmonieux des bateaux qui aient jamais navigué sur les océans ont été conçus par des pirates et des contrebandiers. Pas si étrange. Vitesse et agilité vous donnent toujours l'avantage, que ce soit dans la rue ou sur la mer.

L'origine du mot *clipper* est incertaine. Il y a plusieurs explications. L'une d'entre elles est apparentée au mot « clip » , qui signifie courir ou voler rapidement - juste comme les clippers. Une autre explication est associée à l'étrave du navire, qui est destinée à couper les vagues plutôt que d'avancer péniblement à travers elles. Ainsi, un clipper n'est pas un type particulier de navire. C'est un bateau rapide, facile à manœuvrer et

THE FIRST BRITISH CLIPPER

The *Scottish Maid* was built in 1839. She is often regarded as the first British clipper. She was built to compete with the paddle-steamers on the Aberdeen - London trade. The name of the shipyard was Alexander Hall & Co. In order to get a maximum-speed hull, the shipyard built models and tested them in a water tank with the sole purpose of minimising the water resistance. The *Scottish Maid* was rigged as a two-mast schooner and had the typical bow and stem of a clipper. Her design became a model for many other British ships. The "Aberdeen Clipper Bow" became a household expression, as the shape circumvented the British tonnage laws, allowing the owner to avoid paying tax for part of the cargo.

construit pour une vitesse maximum plutôt que pour une cargaison maximum. Un clipper peut être gréé avec deux ou plusieurs mâts ; il peut-être une petite goélette, un bateau à voiles carrées, un brick ou une barque …

Les noms des plus célèbres clippers en témoignent: *Lightning, Flying Cloud, Ariel, White Squall, Stag Hound, Tornado, Sea Witch …*

(*Eclair, Nuage Volant, Arie, Rafale Blanche, Chien de Chasse, Tornado, Sorcière des Mers…*)

L'âge d'or des clippers a été de courte durée, une vingtaine d'années seulement. Il a commencé à la fin des années 1840 et s'est poursuivi jusqu'au début des années 1870. Les routes du commerce les plus importantes étaient :

1. New York - San Francisco via le Cap Horn. A bord des chercheurs d'or plein d'espoir en route pour faire fortune en Californie.

2. Chine - Angleterre avec des cargaisons de thé. Le capitaine et l'équipage à bord du premier bateau arrivé à Londres pouvaient recevoir des récompenses en extra.

3. Inde - Chine avec de l'opium. L'opium était passé en contrebande en Chine et illégalement échangé contre de l'argent-métal, le seul produit que la Chine acceptait d'échanger contre du thé.

Mais tout avait commencé un siècle plus tôt. Les premiers bateaux que nous pourrions appeler des clippers ont été construits en Bretagne et en Normandie autour des années 1800.

Le mot « clipper » n'existait pas encore mais les bateaux avaient des qualités similaires et une forme de coque qui sera ultérieurement largement connue comme une tête de morue et une queue de maquereau.

Les bateaux français étaient utilisés pour la contrebande et par les corsaires pendant la période de troubles Napoléoniens. Les lourds et gros bateaux armés britanniques étaient une proie facile pour les lévriers des océans. David contre Goliath. Lord Nelson admit à contre-cœur que les meilleures frégates de la marine britannique pendant la guerre contre Napoléon étaient celles qu'il avait prises aux Français. Ces bateaux avaient été dessinés et construits en France !

Les lourds navires de la flotte anglaise ont eu aussi des problèmes pendant la guerre de 1812 contre les Etats-Unis. Le long de la côte est de l'Amérique, était construit un type de bateaux dénommés Clippers de Baltimore. Ils étaient de bons voiliers, légèrement armés et parfaits pour les corsaires. Les Clippers de Baltimore avaient eu du succès contre les Anglais. Quelques décennies plus tard, en 1837, le Parlement Britannique eut une discussion sur ce sujet :

« Les navires américains côtoyant les ports anglais ont été déclarés par plusieurs témoins comme étant supérieurs à des bateaux Anglais de classe similaire. Les commandants et les officiers étant généralement considérés comme les marins et les navigateurs les plus compétents. »

Les navires américains qui ont tant impressionné les Anglais sont ceux qui ont navigué sur des trajets réguliers entre l'Angleterre et les USA. Ils étaient appelés bateaux emballés. Les ports les plus fréquentés étaient Liverpool et New York.

Mais la compétition Américano-Britannique dans la construction des bateaux les plus rapides allait devenir plus intense. En 1845, Donald McKay, un jeune constructeur inventif de navires, commença à dessiner et à construire des bateaux au chantier de Boston.

C'était le début de l'âge d'or, de courte durée, des clippers. L'historien maritime américain

Arthur H Clark dans son grand recueil *The Clipper Slip Era* (1910) déclare non sans un brin de malice :

« Adieu alors aux navires marchands *Indiaman* de la compagnie anglaise des indes orientales, lourdement armés, et leurs équipements encombrants; adieu également à leurs marins, dignes héritiers de ceux qui ont combattu dans la flotte victorieuse de Nelson, qui prenaient une pincée de poudre à canon dans leur rhum avant de se lancer dans la bataille et qui supportaient les caresses du *chat à neuf queues* sans sourciller. »

CHINESE JUNK and tea clipper. Painting by Carl Hendel Friberg

DSCHUNKE und Teeklipper, Gemälde von Carl Hendel Friberg;

JONQUE CHINOISE et clipper de thé. Peinture par Carl Hendel Friberg

DER ERSTE BRITISCHE KLIPPER

Die *Scottish Maid* wurde 1839 gebaut. Sie gilt allgemein als der erste britische Klipper. Man baute sie, um mit den Schaufelraddampfern auf der Route Aberdeen - London zu konkurrieren. Die Werft war Alexander Hall&Co. in Aberdeen. Um zu einer möglichst schnellen Schiffsform zu kommen, baute die Werft Modelle und zog sie durch ein Bassin; alles um den Wasserwiderstand zu minimieren. Die *Scottish Maid* bekam das für die Klipperschiffe typische Vorschiff. Sie wurde dann auch das Modell für viele andere britische Schiffe.

LE PREMIER CLIPPER BRITANNIQUE

Le *Scottish Maid* a été construit en 1839. Il est souvent considéré comme le premier clipper britannique. Il était construit pour faire concurrence aux vapeurs à aubes sur la ligne Aberdeen- Londres. Afin d'obtenir la vitesse maximum de coque, le chantier construisait des maquettes et les testait dans un bassin avec pour seul objectif de minimiser la résistance de l'eau. Le *Scottish Maid* était gréé en goélette à deux mâts et avait une étrave et une proue typique d'un clipper. Son plan devint un modèle pour de nombreux autres bateaux britanniques.

THE WIZARD OF BOSTON

Clipper Lane is the name of a little street, hardly a hundred metres in length, in East Boston, Massachusetts, USA. It was there, or in nearby Border Street, that the fastest and most elegant clipper ships were built in the mid-nineteenth century. The master shipwright was Donald McKay - although he himself would never subscribe to that description, at least not officially. "I am just a mechanic", he said, "but a mechanic with luck. My wife Albenia taught me algebra and trigonometry, the bases for making a construction drawing. And it was not me, but John Griffiths, who designed the sharp bow, narrower midships and full stern. And it was Nathaniel Palmer who developed the flatter hull."

That is correct. Griffith designed the clipper *Rainbow* in 1845. She is often called the first extreme clipper. The following year he built the *Sea Witch*, which in 1850 sailed from New York to San Francisco in the record time of 97 days.

But that record only lasted for a year. In 1851, the *Flying Cloud* made the passage in 89 days and 21 hours, that is almost ten per cent faster. Three years later, the *Flying Cloud* beat her own record. The new passage time was 89 days, 8 hours, which was regarded as unbeatable - and remained so for more than 130 years!

It was Donald McKay (1810-1880) who designed and built the *Flying Cloud*. He had learnt shipbuilding at various shipyards in New York in the 1820's and 30's. In 1845, he moved to Boston.

McKay refined the clipper hull, and all his ships were record-breakers - at a time when record passages were important. The American and British press continuously reported on the newest and fastest ships; a fast ship could get better cargo rates and was more popular with passengers.

But McKay was also a more efficient and quicker builder than other yards. The ships were still built of wood, and the mechanic McKay designed steam-powered cranes, saws and other aids in order to facilitate and speed up production. He succeeded in building forty clippers during the twenty years that he ran the shipyard at Border Street. This was in an era, when fast sailing vessels could still keep an even pace with steamships, and sometimes outsail them. Like in the informal contest between the steamer S/S *Canada* and McKay's *Sovereign of the Seas*. The year was 1853, and McKay himself was on board the clipper. A comparison between the logbooks of the two ships shows that the *Sovereign of the Seas* was on average almost three knots faster during a five-day period.

Donald McKay died in 1880. A park and a school in East Boston are named for him and the Border Street waterfront is still full of timbers, piles, jetties and other relics from the days when the fastest and most elegant ships were built there.

Clipper Lane heißt ein knapp einhundert Meter langes Straßenende in East Boston, Massachusetts, USA. Hier, und gleich nebenan in der Border Street, wurden die schnellsten und schönsten Klipperschiffe in der Mitte des 19. Jahrhunderts gebaut. Der Schiffbaumeister war Donald McKay. Er selbst wäre mit diesem Titel niemals einverstanden gewesen - auf jeden Fall nicht offiziell. „Ich bin nur ein Mechaniker" erklärte er „aber ein Mechaniker mit Glück."

„Meine Frau Albenia brachte mir Algebra und Trigonometrie bei, Voraussetzung für das Erstellen von Konstruktionszeichnungen. Nicht ich entwickelte den scharfen Bug, das schmalere Mittelschiff und das volle Achterschiff, sondern John Griffiths. Und es war Nathanial Palmers, der den flacheren Rumpf einführte."

Das ist eigentlich richtig. Griffiths konstruierte den Klipper *Rainbow* im Jahre 1845. Er gilt allgemein als der erste extreme Klipper. Im Jahr darauf baute er *Sea Witch*, die im Jahre 1850 die Strecke New York-San Francisco in der Rekordzeit von 97 Tagen zurücklegte. Der Rekord hielt allerdings nur für ein Jahr. 1851 segelte die *Flying Cloud* dieselbe Route in 89 Tagen und 21 Stunden, also fast 10% schneller. Drei Jahre später stellte *Flying Cloud* den eigenen Rekord ein. Die neue Zeit war 89 Tage 8 Stunden, was man als unschlagbar ansah - und es blieb auch so für über 130 Jahre!

Es war Donald McKay (1810 - 1880), der die *Flying Cloud* entwarf und baute. Er hatte den Schiffbau auf verschiedenen Werften in New York in den 1820iger und 30iger Jahren gelernt. Im Jahre 1845 zog er nach Boston. McKay verbesserte den Rumpf der Klipper und seine Schiffe schlugen

alle Rekorde - und Rekordzeiten waren damals wichtig. Die amerikanischen und britischen Zeitungen berichteten ständig über die neuesten und schnellsten Schiffe. Ein schnelles Schiff erzielte bessere Fracht-raten und fand leichter Passagiere.

McKay baute auch effektiver und schneller als andere Werften. Die Schiffe wurden noch aus Holz gebaut und der Mechaniker McKay entwickelte dampfgetriebene Kräne und vieles anderes, um die Fertigung zu erleichtern und zu beschleunigen. Es gelang ihm, in den zwanzig Jahren an der Spitze der Werft an der Border Street vierzig Klipperschiffe fertigzustellen.

Es war außerdem eine Zeit, in der schnelle Segler es noch mit den Dampfschiffen aufnehmen konnten - manchmal waren die Segler sogar schneller. So bei dem informellen Wettrennen zwischen dem Dampfschiff *S.S. Canada* und McKay's *Sovereign of the Seas*. Es fand 1853 statt und McKay war selbst an Bord des Klippers. Ein Vergleich der Logbücher der beiden Schiffe zeigt, dass die *Sovereign of the Seas* über einen Zeitraum von fünf Tagen im Schnitt fast drei Knoten schneller war.

Donald McKay starb 1880. Ein Park und eine Schule in East Boston sind nach ihm benannt und das gesamte Ufer entlang der Border Street ist noch heute voll von Holzstammen, Pfahlen, Landungsbrücken und anderen Überresten aus der Zeit, als hier die schnellsten und schönsten Schiffe gebaut wurden.

Clipper Lane est le nom d'une petite rue, de moins de cent mètres de long, à l'est de Boston, dans le Massachusetts, USA. C'est là, ou dans une rue adjacente, que le plus rapide et le plus élégant des clippers a été construit au milieu du 19è siècle.

Le maître constructeur était un certain Donald McKay - même s'il ne s´identifiait pas à ce titre, du moins pas officiellement ; « Je suis juste un mécanicien », disait-il, « mais un mécanicien avec de la chance. Ma femme Albenia m'a appris l'algèbre, la trigonométrie et les bases pour faire les plans d'une construction. C'est John Griffiths, qui a dessiné l'étrave effilée, la coque la plus étroite et la poupe épanouie. Nath Palmer a développé une coque beaucoup plus plate. »

Griffith dessina le clipper *Rainbow* en 1845, souvent désigné comme le premier clipper extrême. L'année suivante il dessina le *Sea Witch*, qui navigua en 1850 de New York à San Francisco dans un temps record de 97 jours.

Mais ce record n'a tenu qu'une année. En 1851, le *Flying Cloud* a fait le trajet en 89 jours et 21 heures, ce qui est presque dix pour cent plus rapide. Trois ans plus tard, le *Flying Cloud* a battu son propre record. Le nouveau temps a été de 89 jours et 8 heures, qui était considéré comme imbattable - et qui a cluré plus de 130 ans!

C'est Donald McKay (1810 - 1880) qui a dessiné et construit le *Flying Cloud*. Il a appris la construction des bateaux dans différents chantiers de New-York dans les années 1820-1830. En 1845 il déménagea à Boston.

McKay affina le dessin de la coque, et tous ses bateaux étaient des plus performants - du temps où les records de traversées étaient importants. La presse américaine et britannique faisait constamment des reportages sur les nouveaux bateaux qui étaient les plus rapides. Grâce à leur vitesse, ces bateaux pouvaient obtenir de meilleurs tarifs de transport ce qui était donc intéressant pour les passagers.

Mais McKay était aussi un constructeur plus efficace et plus rapide que les autres chantiers. Avec les bateaux encore construits en bois McKay dessina des grues à vapeur afin de faciliter et d'accélérer les manutentions. Il réussit à construire quarante clippers pendant les vingt années qu'il a dirigé le chantier de la rue Border.

A cette époque, les bateaux à voiles, pouvaient être encore plus performants que certains bateaux à vapeur - et quelque fois les battre. Comme la course informelle entre le vapeur *S/S Canada* et le clipper *Sovereign of the Seas* en 1853, avec McKay à bord du clipper.

La comparaison entre les livres de bord des deux navires montre que le *Sovereign of the Seas* a été, en moyenne, trois nœuds plus rapide pendant une période de cinq jours.

Donald McKay mourut en 1880. Un parc et une école de l'est de Boston portent son nom et la rue Border au bord de l'eau, est encore pleine de bois de construction, de jetées et autres reliques du temps où les plus rapides et les plus élégants des bateaux étaient construits.

DONALD MCKAY.
Daguerreotype.

DONALD MCKAY.
Daguerreotypie.

DONALD MCKAY.
Daguerréotype.

1849 THE RUSH IS ON

It is 1847, and San Francisco has a few hundred inhabitants. The shabby little village is visited by some ten ships a year. On the 24th of January next year, everything is changed. That day, James William Marshall strikes gold in the American River in California. When the New York Herald reports on the find, the great gold rush to the West starts. At this time, there are three ways of going from the American east coast to the west coast.

- On a sailing ship around South America via Cape Horn. The distance is 16,000 nautical miles (18,000 statute miles or 30,000 kilometres).
- By foot or horse-drawn wagon across the American continent. The distance is 3,000 miles (4,700 kilometres).
- By sea to the Isthmus of Panama, by foot across to the Pacific, and then by sea again.

There were great dangers involved in all the three routes. Gales at Cape Horn, unfriendly Indians in the Wild West and deadly diseases in the swamps of the Isthmus of Panama. Most of the adventurers chose to board a ship and sail the entire route.

Already, in the year after Marshall's strike, 775 ships had anchored in San Francisco Bay, compared with some ten the year before. 90,000 gold diggers came to California in the first year.

The demand for ships was enormous, and the East Coast shipyards built 160 new clipper ships during the first four Gold Rush years. Many of the ships got stuck in San Francisco after the first voyage. Their crews ran off to find gold. The ships became wrecks or storages, shops, hotels, bars, brothels or prisons.

For the shipowners, the New York - San Francisco route was splendid business. Besides the fares paid by the gold diggers, they had earnings from the ships' cargoes of everything that the gold diggers could need, from flour to whiskey, clothes, buckets and shovels… What could be bought in New York for a dollar could be sold in San Francisco for ten.

One of the early arrivals was a tailor from Bavaria in Germany. His name was Levi Strauss, and he came to San Francisco in 1853. He sewed trousers of old tarpaulin and fixed the pockets with copper rivets. Levi Strauss was to earn considerably more money from his Levis jeans than the gold diggers would get for the gold nuggets that they washed out.

Wir sind im Jahre 1847 und San Francisco hat ein paar hundert Einwohner. Nur an die zehn Schiffe finden jedes Jahr den Weg zu dem hässlichen kleinen Dorf. Am 24. Januar des folgenden Jahres ändert sich alles. James William Marshall findet Gold im American River in Kalifornien. Als die Zeitung New York Herald von dem Fund berichtet, bricht im Westen der große Goldrausch aus.

Zu dieser Zeit gibt es drei Möglichkeiten von der amerikanischen Ostküste an die Westküste zu kommen: 1. Mit dem Segelschiff rund um Südamerika vorbei an Kap Horn. Das sind 16 000 Seemeilen (30 000 km). 2. Zu Fuß oder mit Pferd und Wagen über den amerikanischen Kontinent, das sind 3 000 Meilen (4 700 km). 3. Mit dem Schiff zur Panama Landenge, zu Fuß zur Pazifischen Küste und danach wieder weiter per Schiff.

Alle drei Wege sind mit großen Gefahren verbunden, Stürme am Kap Horn, feindliche Indianer im Wilden Westen und tödliche Krankheiten in den Sümpfen von Panama. Die meisten Abenteurer wählten das Schiff und segelten die gesamte Strecke.

WASHING-PAN. The most important tool for a gold-digger. 1860.

DIE PFANNE, wichtigstes Gerät der Golfgräber. 1860.

PLATEAU DE SÉDIMENTATION. L'outil le plus important pour un chercheur d'or. 1860.

THE FIRST ADVERTISING WAR

The competition between the ships was tough. Speed was more important than comfort. The newspapers reported on record voyages, and shipowners and agents started the first modern advertisement war: "A New and Magnificent Clipper for San Francisco. Unusually prompt and a very quick trip may be relied upon." The advertisement also states that the ship is moored and waiting at Pier 13, East River. "Engagements should be completed at once."

Schon ein Jahr nach Marshalls Entdeckung gingen 775 Schiffe in der Bucht von San Francisco vor Anker; verglichen mit rund 10 im Jahre vorher. 90 000 Goldgräber kamen im ersten Jahr in den „Golden State". Der Bedarf an Schiffen war enorm und die Werften an der amerikanischen Ostküste bauten in den ersten vier Jahren des Goldrausches 160 neue Klipperschiffe.

Viele der Schiffe blieben nach der ersten Reise in San Francisco liegen, weil die Besatzungen auf Goldsuche gingen. Die Schiffe verfielen oder verwandelten sich in Geschäfte, Hotels, Bars, Bordelle und Gefängnisse. Für die Reeder war die Fahrt New York - San Francisco ein glänzendes Geschäft. Außer den Fahrpreisen, die die Goldgräber bezahlten, nahm man noch alles mit, was die Goldgräber benötigen könnten, von Mehl bis Whiskey, Bekleidung, Eimer und Spaten...

Was man in New York für einen Dollar einkaufen konnte, ließ sich in San Francisco für das Zehnfache verkaufen. Einer der frühen Ankömmlinge war ein Schneider aus Bayern. Sein Name war Levi Strauss und er kam im Jahre 1853 nach San Francisco. Aus altem Segeltuch nähte er Hosen für die Goldgräber und befestigte die Taschen mit Kupfernieten. Levi Strauss sollte wesentlich mehr mit seinen Levi Jeans verdienen als die Goldgräber mit den Goldnuggets, die sie aus dem Fluss gewaschen hatten.

En 1847, San Francisco ne compte qu'une centaines d'habitants. Le pauvre petit village recevait la visite d'une dizaine de bateaux par an. Le 24 janvier de l'année suivante, tout a changé. Ce jour-là, James William Marshall découvre de l'or dans la rivière Américaine en Californie. Quand l'Herald de New York a dévoilé la découverte, la grande ruée vers l'ouest a commencé. En ce temps-là, il y avait trois façons d'aller de la côte est de l'Amérique à la côte ouest: 1. Sur un bateau à voile en faisant le tour de l'Amérique via le Cap Horn. La distance est de 16 000 milles nautiques (18 000 miles routiers - 30 000 km). 2. A pied ou dans un charriot tiré par un cheval à travers le continent américain. La distance est de 3 000 miles (4 700 km). 3. Par mer jusqu'au Détroit de Panama, à pied jusqu'au Pacifique, et à nouveau par la mer.

Les trois routes comportaient de grands dangers. Des coups de vent au Cap Horn, des Indiens redoutables dans le centre ouest et des maladies mortelles dans les marais du détroit de Panama. La plupart des aventuriers ont choisi de voyager à bord d'un bateau pour le trajet entier.

Presqu'un an après la découverte de Marshall, 775 bateaux ont ancré dans la baie de San Francisco, contre une dizaine l'année précédente.

90 000 chercheurs d'or arrivèrent en Californie la première année.

La demande de bateaux était énorme et les chantiers de la côte est construisirent 160 nouveaux clippers pendant les quatre premières années de la Ruée vers l'Or. Un grand nombre de ces bateaux restèrent à San Francisco après leur premier voyage. Leurs équipages s'enfuirent pour chercher de l'or.

Les bateaux devinrent des épaves ou des entrepôts, des magasins, des hôtels, des bars, des bordels ou des prisons.

Pour les armateurs, la route de New York - San Francisco était une affaire magnifique. En plus des billets payés par les chercheurs d'or, ils avaient des marges sur toutes les marchandises embarquées dont pouvaient avoir besoin les chercheurs d'or, depuis la farine jusqu'au whiskey, vêtements, seaux... Tout ce qui pouvait être acheté à New York pour un dollar, pouvait être vendu à San Francisco à dix dollars.

L'un des premiers arrivés, en 1853, était un tailleur de Bavière en Allemagne. Son nom était Levi Strauss. Il confectionnait des pantalons avec de vieilles bâches et fixait les poches avec des rivets en cuivre. Levi Strauss a gagné une quantité considérable d'argent, bien plus importante avec ses jeans Levis que les chercheurs d'or avaient obtenu des pépites d'or qu'ils avaient extrait par lavage du sable.

SAN FRANCISCO in 1851. Daguerrotype.

SAN FRANCISCO 1851. Daguerrotypie.

SAN FRANCISCO en 1851. Daguerréotype.

DER ERSTE ANZEIGENKRIEG

Die Konkurrenz zwischen den Schiffen war hart. Die Geschwindigkeit war wichtiger als der Komfort. Die Zeitungen berichteten über Rekordfahrten und die Reedereien begannen den ersten Anzeigenkrieg.
„Ein neuer großartiger Clipper nach San Francisco. Eine ungewöhnlich prompte und schnelle Reise ist garantiert." Die Annonce lockte auch damit, dass das Schiff am Pier 13, East River, New York lag und wartete. „Buchungen sollten unverzüglich erfolgen."

LA PREMIERE GUERRE PUBLICITAIRE

La compétition entre les bateaux était enclenchée. La vitesse était bien plus importante que le confort. La presse faisait le scoop de chaque grand record de vitesse. C'est de là que la première guerre publicitaire commençait entre les armateurs et leurs agents.
« Un magnifique Clipper neuf et très rapide pour San Francisco». La publicité rajoutait que le navire est à quai et attend au quai 13, East River:
« Les formulaires d'embarquement peuvent être complétés immédiatement. »

Such glorious eyes I never saw, large liquid and hazel, soft as a gazelle´s and always beaming with kindness on someone." The name of the girl with the glorious eyes was Ellen Creesy, and the description of her eyes and her kindness is from a letter, written on board the clipper *Flying Cloud* on her maiden voyage from New York to San Francisco in 1851. It was written by Sarah Bowman, a passenger. It might as well have been written today, on one of the Star Clipper ships, as most of the letter deals with sunsets, how passengers were dressed, what they drank and whom they flirted with.

But this is not any voyage, and Ellen was a very important person on board. She was navigating the *Flying Cloud* the 16,000 nautical miles to San Francisco. She was the one who selected the routes which made the *Flying Cloud* sail faster than any other ship between the American east and west coasts. In 1851, it took 89 days and 21 hours. Three years later, it was still faster - 89 days and 8 hours. The normal passage time in this age was 100 days or more.

Ellen was born in 1814 to a shipping family in Marblehead, Massachusetts. She was a Dad's girl and at an early age learnt all about navigation. At 27, in 1841, she married. Her husband was Captain Perkins Creesy, and their honeymoon was of course celebrated on board a sailing ship. Ellen then sailed as a navigator together with her husband on all the world's seas.

The couple spent far more time together on board than ashore. When Perkins got the command of the new *Flying Cloud*, it was self-evident that Ellen would be on board. She brought with her the new book by the oceanographer Matthew Fontaine Maury:

"Explanations and Sailing Directions to Accompany the Wind and Current Charts".

Maury's book provided new knowledge about currents, waves and winds, and eventually it became indispensable for all navigators. But in 1851, this was new knowledge, and Ellen was one of the first to make efficient use of it.

The only way of determining one's position at that time was by astronomical navigation, observing the sun, the moon or the stars. In cloudy or bad weather, dead reckoning was used, combining the ship's speed and course with the effects of wind, waves and currents. It is all a combination of mathematics and feeling - and Ellen mastered both.

When, in the afternoon of July 31st, she sat down to calculate the last 24-hour distance, she hardly believed her own figures. 374 nautical miles. She calculated once more, but arrived at the same result. 374 miles in 24 hours means an average speed of approximately 15 knots. No other ship had sailed that fast before.

When she told her husband, he embraced her - at least according to the author David W. Shaw, who wrote a book about the record voyage.

Nie habe ich solch wunderschöne Augen gesehen, groß und braun, sanft wie die einer Gazelle und immer mit einem freundlichen Blick für jemanden". Die Frau mit den wunderschönen Augen hieß Ellen Creesy und die Beschreibung ihrer Augen und Freundlichkeit findet sich in einem Brief wieder, der im Jahre 1851 an Bord des Klippers *Flying Cloud* während der Jungfernfahrt zwischen New York - San Francisco geschrieben wurde. Der Verfasser des Briefes war ein Passagier namens Sarah Bowman. Der Brief hätte genauso gut heute an Bord eines der Segler von Star Clippers geschrieben werden können. Ansonsten handelt der Brief meistens von Sonnen-untergängen, der Mode der Passagiere, Trinkge-wohnheiten und kleinen Flirts. Aber dies ist nicht eine Segelfahrt wie jede andere.

Ellen war eine wichtige Person an Bord. Sie war Navigator für die 16 000 Seemeilen bis San Francisco. Sie wählte die Route aus, die die *Flying Cloud* schneller als jedes andere Schiff zwischen der Ost- und Westküste der USA segeln ließ. Im Jahre 1851 dauerte die Überfahrt 89 Tage und 31 Stunden. Im Jahre 1854, drei Jahre später, ging es noch schneller, 89 Tage und 8 Stunden. Ansonsten waren damals 100 Tage oder mehr üblich.

Ellen wurde 1814 in eine Seemannsfamilie in Marblehead, Massachusetts, geboren. Sie war die Lieblingstochter ihres Vaters und lernte frühzeitig alles über die Navigation. Im Alter von 27 Jahren heiratete sie den Kapitän Perkins Creesy und die Hochzeitsreise fand natürlich auf einem Segelschiff statt. Danach begleitete Ellen ihren Ehemann als

Navigator auf allen Weltmeeren. Die beiden verbrachten mehr Zeit zur See als auf dem Land. Als Perkins 1851 Kapitän auf der neugebauten *Flying Cloud* wurde, befand sich selbstverständlich auch Ellen an Bord. Bei sich hatte sie das gerade herausgegebene Buch des Ozeanographen Matthew Fontain Maury: „*Explanations and Sailing Directions to Accompany the Wind and Current Charts*". (Erläuterungen und Segelanweisungen zur Begleitung der Karten von Wind und Strömungen).

Maurys Buch lieferte neue Erkenntnisse über Strömungen, Wellen und Wind. Nach und nach wurde es unverzichtbar für alle Navigatoren, aber 1851 war es eine neue Erkenntnis und Ellen war eine der Ersten, die diese mit Erfolg anwendete. Zur damaligen Zeit konnte man eine sichere Position nur durch astronomische Navigation und durch Beobachtung von Sonne, Mond oder Sternen bestimmen.

Bei Wolken oder schlechtem Wetter verließ man sich auf die laufende Ortsbestimmung, bei der man die Fahrt des Schiffes, Wellen, Strömungen, Windrichtung und Kurs zusammen berücksichtigen musste. Alles ist eine Kombination von Mathematik und Gefühl - und Ellen besaß beides.

Als sie sich am Nachmittag des 31. Juli hinsetzte, um die zurückgelegte Entfernung des letzten Tages zu berechnen, traute sie ihren eigenen Zahlen nicht. Sie rechnete noch einmal nach, kam aber zu demselben Ergebnis. 374 Seemeilen in 24 Stunden sind im Schnitt ungefähr 15,5 Knoten. So schnell war bis dahin kein Segelschiff gefahren. Als sie dies ihrem Mann berichtete, wurde sie von ihm umarmt - auf jeden Fall laut Bericht des Verfassers David W. Shaw, der ein Buch über die Rekordfahrt schrieb.

Des yeux si beaux, couleur noisette comme ceux d'une gazelle, grands, limpides et remplis d'une bienveillance, comme je n'en avais jamais vu ». Le nom de la fille aux yeux magnifiques était Ellen Creesy. La description de ses yeux et sa gentilesse a été écrite dans une lettre, rédigée à bord du clipper *Flying Cloud* au cours de son premier voyage de New York à San Francisco en 1851.

Elle a été écrite par une passagère prénommée Sarah Bowman. Cela aurait pu être écrit aujourd'hui sur l'un des bateaux de Star Clippers. La plus grande partie de la lettre parle de couchers de soleil, de la manière dont les passagers sont habillés, ce qu'ils boivent et avec qui ils flirtent.

Mais ce n'était pas n'importe quel voyage, et Ellen était une personne très importante à bord. Elle naviguait sur le *Flying Cloud* pour les 16 000 nautiques jusqu'à San Francisco. Et elle était la personne qui choisissait les routes qui permettaient au *Flying Cloud* de naviguer plus vite que n'importe quel autre bateau entre la côte est de l'Amérique et la côte ouest. En 1851, cela prenait 89 jours et 21 heures. Trois ans plus tard, il allait encore plus vite - 89 jours et 8 heures. Le temps normal à cette epoque était de 100 jours ou plus.

Elle était née en 1814 dans une famille d'armateurs à Malblehead, Massachusetts. Elle était la fille à son père et dès son plus jeune âge elle a tout appris sur la navigation. A 27 ans, en 1841, elle se maria. Son mari était le Capitaine Perkins Creesy, et leur lune de miel bien entendu a été célébrée à bord d'un bateau à voile. Ellen a ensuite navigué comme Capitaine avec son mari sur toutes les mers du monde.

Le couple a passé beaucoup plus de temps ensemble à bord qu'à terre. Lorsque Perkings fût nommé Capitaine, du nouveau *Flying Cloud*, Ellen l'accompagna comme navigatrice.

Elle emporta avec elle le nouveau livre de l'océanographe Matthew Fontaine Maury:

« *Explanations and Sailing Directions to Accompany the Wind and Current Charts* ». Le livre de Maury fournissait de nouvelles connaissances sur les courants, les vagues et les vents, et devenait finalement indispensable à tous les navigateurs. Cependant en 1851, c'était tout nouveau, et Ellen a été l'une des premières à s'en servir efficacement.

La seule façon de déterminer sa position en ce temps-là, était la navigation astronomique, en observant le soleil, la lune ou les étoiles. Par temps nuageux ou par mauvais temps, le calcul était pratiqué avec un loch, combiné avec la vitesse du bateau et bien sûr avec les effets du vent, des vagues et des courants. Cela tient en une combinaison de règles mathématiques et des sens - et Ellen les maîtrisait tous les deux.

L'après-midi du 31 juillet, elle s'assit pour calculer la distance des dernières 24 heures, elle ne pouvait croire ses propres chiffres.

Elle refit ses calculs une nouvelle fois et elle arriva au même résultat. 374 miles nautiques en 24 heures ce qui veut dire une vitesse moyenne d'environ 15,5 nœuds. Pas un seul bateau n'avait naviguer aussi vite auparavant. Quand elle en informa son mari, il l'embrassa - selon l'auteur David W. Show, qui écrivait un livre à propos du voyage record.

THE FLYING CLOUD *sailed faster than any other ship.*

DIE FLYING CLOUD *war schneller als jedes andere Schiff.*

LE FLYING CLOUD *a navigué plus vite que n'importe quel autre bateau.*

CAPTAIN KEAY ON THE ARIEL

"*Ariel* was a perfect beauty to every nautical man who saw her; in symmetrical grace and proportion of hull, spars, sails, rigging and finish, she satisfied the eye and put all in love with her without exception. The curve of stem, figurehead and entrance, the easy sheer and graceful lines of the hull seemed grown and finished as life takes shape and beauty; it was a pleasure to coach her. In fact, she could do everything short of speaking."

KAPITÄN KEAY ÜBER ARIEL

„*Ariel* war für alle Seeleute die vollendete Schönheit. Alle verliebten sich in die harmonische Eleganz und das Zusammenspiel zwischen Rumpf, Aufbauten, Takelage, Segel und Ausführung. Der Bogen des Stevens, die Galionsfigur und das graziöse Linienspiel erschienen entstanden und vollendet zu sein wie das Leben selbst. Es war eine Freude, sie zu führen. Sie vermochte wirklich alles außer sprechen."

CAPITAINE KEAY SUR L`ARIEL

« *L'Ariel* était d'une beauté parfaite; par sa grâce symétrique et les proportions de sa coque, ses épars, ses voiles, son gréement et ses finitions, il avait une ligne magnifique et tout le monde en tombait amoureux. Les lignes de l'étrave, et de la proue, l'avant les lignes pures et gracieuses de la coque, tout le rendait exceptionnel et vraiment il ne lui manquait que la parole. »

1866 THE PERFECT RACE

Late in May, 1866, the tea clipper *Ariel* had taken on a full cargo. She was anchored on the Min River north of Hong Kong. On board were 523 tons of tea, neatly packed in chests, lined with oiled paper. The chests were painted and sealed with lead plate. Next to the *Ariel* were two more clippers, *Taeping* and *Serica*, also carrying tea cargoes. The challenge was to be the first to arrive in London.

In mid 19th century England drinking tea was high fashion, and the London tea merchants were waiting eagerly. To make the captains push ships and crews to the utmost, the owners were offering a special reward of 10 shillings per ton to the ship that arrived first. Additionally, the winning captain was to be rewarded with 100 pounds and the officers and crew with an extra month's wages. The three ships weighed anchor and set sail on the same tide. On the 30th of May, the famous tea race of 1866 got under way.

Three months later, there was great excitement in London. The brokers were preparing themselves. Which ship would be the first? On September 5th, the telegraph ticked in London.

At sunrise, six o'clock, there had been a sighting at The Lizard, the southernmost point of England. Not one, but two ships had been seen: *Ariel* and *Taeping*. At about the same time the two captains, John Keay on the *Ariel* and Donald MacKinnon on the *Taeping* had sighted each other. This was the start of a furious race up the Channel, with the Dungeness pilots as the first goal. The next challenge was to be first to reach a tug at the entrance to the Thames estuary. It was impossible to go up the meandering river under sail.

The *Ariel*, named after the airy spirit in Shakespeare's The Tempest, was ahead. She flew along the choppy English Channel with all her sails set - 39 of them! *Ariel* reached a tug eight minutes ahead of *Taeping*, but *Taeping's* tug was faster. At 9.45 pm on the 6th of September, *Taeping* moored in the old London Docks. *Ariel* tied up in the East India Docks 38 minutes later. So small was the time difference after 99 days of sailing. And what happened to the reward? The owners decided to split it evenly between the two ships. What of the third ship, *Serica*, which had left China on the same tide? She arrived hardly more than an hour after *Ariel*!

Ende Mai 1866 war der Teeklipper *Ariel* voll beladen. Das Schiff lag vor Anker auf dem Fluss Minkiang nördlich von Hongkong. An Bord befanden sich 523 Tonnen Tee, sauber verpackt in Kisten, die mit Ölpapier ausgelegt waren. Die Kisten waren gestrichen und mit Blei versiegelt. Gleich neben der *Ariel* ankerten zwei weitere Teeklipper, *Taeping* und *Serica*. Sie hatten ebenfalls Tee geladen. Jetzt ging es darum, zuerst nach London zu kommen.

Teetrinken war Mitte des 19. Jahrhunderts die große Mode in England und Londons Teehändler warteten gespannt. Um die Kapitäne dazu zu bringen, Schiff und Mannschaft auf das äußerste anzutreiben, setzten die Reeder eine extra Belohnung für das am ersten einlaufende Schiff aus. Die drei Schiffe lichteten den Anker und setzten Segel mit derselben Tide. Es war der 30. Mai. Das Rennen von 1866 hatte begonnen.

Drei Monate später war die Spannung in London groß. Die Schiffsmakler machten sich bereit. Welches Schiff würde zuerst gesichtet werden. Am 5. September ratterten die Telegraphen in London. Um 6 Uhr, gerade bei Sonnenaufgang, waren bei Lizard, Englands südlichstem Punkt, Schiffe gesichtet worden; nicht eins, sondern zwei: *Ariel* und *Taeping*. Ungefähr zur gleichen Zeit hatten auch Kapitän John Keay auf der *Ariel* und Donald MacKinnon auf der *Taeping* einander gesichtet.

Jetzt begann ein wahnwitziges Rennen durch den Ärmelkanal mit den Lotsen bei Dungeness als erstes Ziel. Dann galt es, den ersten Schlepper in der Themsemündung zu erreichen. Es war unmöglich, die siebzig Seemeilen die Themse hinauf zu segeln.

Ariel, die nach dem Luftgeist in Shakespears Komödie „The Tempest" benannt war, lag vorn. Sie flog über den rauen Ärmelkanal mit allen Segeln gesetzt - 39 an der Zahl. *Ariel* nahm den Schlepper acht Minuten früher als *Taeping*, aber *Taepings* Schlepper war schneller. Um 21:45 am 6. September lag die *Taeping* vertäut in den London Docks. *Ariel* legte in den East India Docks 38 Minuten später an. So gering war also der Zeitunterschied nach 99 Tagen Segeln. Und was passierte mit der Belohnung? Die Reeder beschlossen, sie zu gleichen Teilen an die zwei Schiffe zu geben.

Fin mai 1866, le clipper transporteur de thé *Ariel* a embarqué une cargaison complète. Il était ancré sur la rivière Min au nord de Hong Kong. A bord, il y avait 523 tonnes de thé, empaquetées d'une manière soignée dans des caisses, tapissées avec du papier huilé. Les caisses étaient peintes et scellées avec des plaques de plomb. A côté de *l'Ariel* il y avait deux autres clippers, le *Taeping* et le *Serica*, transportant eux aussi du thé. Le challenge était alors d'arriver le premier à Londres.

En Angleterre, au milieu du 19è siècle, boire du thé était à la mode, et les marchands de thé londoniens attendaient ces bateaux avec impatience. Afin de motiver les capitaines à pousser les vaisseaux et leurs équipages à leur maximum, les armateurs offraient une prime spéciale de 10 shillings par tonne au bateau qui arriverait le premier. En plus, le capitaine vainqueur, recevrait une prime de 100 livres et les officiers et l'équipage un mois de salaire supplémentaire. Les trois navires levèrent l'ancre et mirent les voiles en même temps. Le 30 mai, la fameuse course du thé commença.

Trois mois plus tard, il y avait une grande agitation à Londres. Quel vaisseau sera le premier à arriver? Le 5 septembre, le télégraphe cliqueta. Au coucher de soleil, à six heures, il y a eu un signe au cap Lizard. Pas un, mais deux bateaux ont été vus: *l'Ariel* et le *Taeping*. A peu près au même moment, John Keay sur *l'Ariel* et Donald MacKinnon sur le *Taeping* se sont aperçus. Ce fut le commencement d'une course furieuse. Le défi était d'atteindre le premier le point de halage à l'entrée de l'estuaire de la Tamise. Il était impossible de remonter la rivière, sous voile.

L'Ariel, dénommé dans l'esprit insouciant de Shakespeare "La Tempête", était en tête. Il volait le long de la Manche agitée, toutes voiles dehors - 39 au total! *L'Ariel* atteignit un point de halage huit minutes avant *Taeping*, mais le halage de *Taeping* était plus rapide. A 21 h 45, le 6 septembre, *Taeping* était amarré le long des vieux quais de Londres. *Ariel* était aux quais de l'Inde de l'Est 38 minutes plus tard.

La différence de temps était tellement faible après 99 jours de navigation. Et qu'en fut-il de la récompense ? Les armateurs décidèrent de la partager en parts égales entre les deux vaisseaux.

THE TAEPING and the *Ariel* in the Channel. *Illustrated London News* 1866.

DIE TEAPING und die *Ariel* im Ärmelkanal. *Illustrated London News* 1866.

LE TAEPING et l'Ariel dans la Manche. *Illustrated London News* 1866.

Iron Men
In Wooden Boats

FOUR *months at sea. Four hours of sleep. Four hours of work. Gale. Heat. Cold. Everything always damp. A seaman's life was tough - and yet there was a flourishing romanticization of life at sea.*

VIER *Monate auf See. Vier Stunden Schlaf. Vier Stunden Dienst. Sturm, Wärme, Kälte, ständige Feuchtigkeit. Das Leben eines Seemanns war extrem hart - trotzdem blühte die Segelromantik.*

QUATRE *mois en mer. Quatre heures de sommeil. Quatre heures de travail. Coups de vent. Chaleur. Froid. Les affaires toujours humides. La vie d'un marin était extrêmement dure - et malgré tout la vie à bord était d'un romantisme florissant.*

WET AND WILD

H e loved her one day and loathed her the next. When he was at sea, he despised it. When in port, he longed for the sea. He had been fifty-five years afloat. I never heard him say that he liked any place he had been to - they were either too damned hot or too damned cold."

Henry Hughes tells of an encounter with the sailor John Davies in his book "Through Mighty Seas". Shipboard life is full of contrasts. On the one hand hard work and lack of sleep, and on the other hand a rosy sunset in a mild trade wind, a romantic seaman's ballad on the fo'c'sle deck, accompanied by a Magdeburger accordion or a moment for yourself by your seaman's chest. The tough and the romantic lives at sea co-existed - and maybe they still do.

In 1905, the Australian Jack McLaren was seventeen and signed on a barque in Australia. In his

book with the revealing title "Blood on the Deck" (1933), he describes the appalling life on board. But also unforgettable moments:

"There were early mornings when from aloft I saw the sun rise as a clear sun that first laid a fan rib design of rays upon the water, then tipped the mast tops with gold in which was a blend of silver, and shone itself directly in my face as though looking at me, examining me perhaps.

There was a high satisfaction that came from the fact that we were wind driven, not machinery driven, that we were making use in the most direct and positive manner of a mighty natural force."

This is how a crew member or a guest on board Star Clippers might describe a sunrise, while the ship is underway from the Canaries to the Caribbean.

On board, the crew was divided into two watches - the starboard and the port watch. Each

watch worked for four hours and rested for four - around the clock (incidentally, the same schedule still applies in many ships). The ship's bell was used for marking the time, the mate striking the bell every half hour. Thus, after four hours, eight bells are struck and it is time for changing the watches. In order to prevent the same men from keeping the same watch each day, the watch between 4 pm and 8 pm was divided into two, known as the first and last dog watches, in order to produce an odd number of watches in each day. Those who took up their watch at 4 pm thus only worked until 6 and then had a free watch until 8, when they again started working.

The clipper crews were almost always of many nationalities and a motley collection of experienced sailors and scum, collected in harbour bars. The latter group is described by the American maritime historian Arthur H Clark:

THE SEAS roll over the deck, when the ship is fully loaded.

DAS WASSER bricht über das Deck bei schwerer Fracht.

LES VAGUES déferlent sur le pont, quand le bateau est à pleine charge.

"To talk about the exercise of kindness or moral suasion with such men, would be the limit of foolishness; one might as well propose a kindergarten for baby coyotes or young rattlesnakes." Clark also gives an amusing, although not necessarily altogether true, description of seamen from various cultures:

"The Liverpool Irishmen" he says, "are wild men, strong, coarse-built, thick-set; their hairy bodies and limbs tattooed with grotesque and often obscene devices in red and blue India ink."

"The packet rats", the Americans manning the clippers on the California trade, were of the same calibre:

"Tough roustabout sailormen and difficult to handle, so that it was sometimes a toss-up whether they or the captain and officers would have charge of the ship". And Clark continues:

"Then there were Spaniards, Portuguese, Chinamen, Frenchmen, Africans, Russians, and Italians from the general merchant service, many of whom were excellent seamen and some of whom were not; and lastly came the men of various nationalities who were not sailors at all nor the stuff out of which sailors could be made, and who had no business to be before the mast on board of a ship."

The only ones who get a really good mark of approval by Clark are the Scandinavians:

"Fine seamen, clean, willing, and obedient, were the first and best class among the men of whom the clipper ship crews were composed."

The internationally renowned Danish author Carsten Jensen summarizes life on board the clippers:

"The only people today who lead a life as exposed as that of a 19th century seaman is a professional soldier in combat."

Er liebte sie den einen Tag, er verachtete sie am nächsten. Wenn er auf dem Meer war, hasste er es. Im Hafen sehnte er sich nach dem Meer. Er war fünfundfünfzig Jahre zur See gefahren. Ich hörte ihn niemals sagen, dass ihm ein Ort gefiel. Es war entweder zu verdammt warm oder zu verdammt kalt."

Harry Huges berichtet von einer Begegnung mit dem Seemann John Davies in dem Buch: „Through Mighty Seas". Das Leben an Bord war voll von Kontrasten. Auf der einen Seite harte Arbeit und Mangel an Schlaf, auf der anderen Seite ein rosig schimmernder Sonnenuntergang in einem lauen Passatwind, eine romantische Seemannsweise an Deck begleitet von einer Ziehharmonika oder eine Weile allein mit der Seemannskiste. Das harte und das romantische Leben auf See existierten Seite an Seite und tun dies vielleicht

STAND BY
in braces and sheets!

KLAR BEI
Brassen und Schoten!

SE TENIR paré entre les entretoises et les écoutes!

auch heute noch. Der Australier Jack McLaren war 17 Jahre alt als er im Jahre 1905 auf einer Bark in Australien anheuerte. In dem Buch mit dem aufschlussreichen Titel „Blood on the Deck" (1933) beschreibt er das widrige Leben an Bord, aber auch unvergessliche Momente: „In den frühen Morgenstunden sah ich die Sonne aufsteigen, die erst ein strahlenförmiges Muster auf das Wasser legte, dann die Mastspitze mit einer Mischung aus Gold und Silber färbte, und direkt in mein Gesicht schien, so als ob sie mich ansah, ja vielleicht prüfte. Es gab eine hohe Genugtuung aus der Tatsache, dass wir vom Wind angetrieben wurden, nicht von einer Maschine; dass wir uns auf eine direkte und positive Weise eine gewaltige Kraft der Natur zu Nutze machten." So könnte ein Besatzungsmitglied oder ein Gast an Bord der Star Clippers einen Sonnenaufgang beschreiben, wenn das Schiff mit Kurs von den Kanarischen Inseln zur Karibik segelt.

Die Besatzung an Bord wurde in zwei Wachen aufgeteilt, Steuerbord Wache und Backbord Wache. Jede Wache arbeitete vier Stunden und ruhte vier Stunden, rund um den ganzen Tag (das gleiche Schema findet sich auch heute noch auf vielen Schiffen). Die Zeit wurde mit Hilfe der Schiffsuhr angezeigt. Der Steuermann markierte jede halbe Stunde mit einem Glockenschlag. Nach vier Stunden waren es also acht Schläge und Wachablösung. Damit dieselbe Wache nicht Ruhe und Arbeit zur selben Zeit an jedem Tag hatte, teilte man die Wache zwischen vier und acht Uhr in zwei Hälften. Wer um vier Uhr auf Wache ging, arbeitete nur bis sechs Uhr - dann gab es die Freiwache für zwei Stunden und die neue Wache begann um acht Uhr.

Die Besatzung auf einem Klipperschiff bestand fast immer aus vielen verschiedenen Nationalitäten und einer Mischung aus erfahrenen Seeleuten und Gesindel, das man in Hafenkneipen zusammengesucht hatte. Die letztere Kategorie beschreibt der Marinehistoriker Arthur H Clark wie folgt:

„Bei solchen Menschen von der Ausübung von Freund-lichkeit oder moralischer Überzeugung zu sprechen, wäre der Gipfel an Dummheit, man könnte genauso gut einen Kindergarten für Kojotenwelpen oder junge Klapperschlangen vorschlagen."

Der Amerikaner Clark gibt auch ein unterhaltsames, wenn vielleicht nicht immer ganz richtiges Bild der Seeleute aus den unterschiedlichen Kulturen: „Die Iren aus Liverpool" sagt er „sind wilde Männer, stark, grob gebaut und kräftig, ihre behaarten Körper sind oft mit grotesken und oft obszönen Motiven in roter und blauer Tinte tätowiert"

The packet rats, die Amerikaner, die die Klipperschiffe auf dem Weg nach Kalifornien bemannten, waren von derselben Sorte: „Zähe Seeleute und schwer zu führen, so dass manchmal nicht klar war, ob sie oder der Kapitän und die Offiziere die Leitung des Schiffes hatten." Und weiter schreibt Clark: „Dann gab es Spanier, Portugiesen, Chinesen, Franzosen, Afrikaner, Russen und Italiener aus der Handelsmarine, von denen viele exzellente Seeleute waren, manche allerdings auch nicht; zuletzt waren da die Vertreter verschiedener Nationen, die wirklich keine Seeleute waren, und aus denen man auch keine Seeleute machen konnte, die kein Recht hatten an Bord eines Schiffes zu sein."

Die Skandinavier sind die einzigen, die von Clark ein gutes Zeugnis erhalten: „Hervorragende Seeleute, willig und gehorsam, waren die erste und beste Klasse von Männer, aus denen die Besatzungen der Klipperschiffe bestanden."

Der international bekannte dänische Verfasser Carsten Jensen fasst das Leben auf den Klipperschiffen wie folgt zusammen: „Die einzigen Menschen heutzutage, die ein ähnlich gefährliches Leben führen wie ein Seemann des 19. Jahrhunderts, sind Berufssoldaten im Kampfeinsatz."

U n jour il aimait la mer et le lendemain il la détestait. Quand il était en mer, il la méprisait. Au port, il en avait la nostalgie. Il a navigué pendant 55 ans et jamais je ne l'ai entendu dire du bien de tous les endroits qu'il avait visités au cours de sa carrière, ils étaient soit trop chauds, soit trop froids. »

THE WHOLE CREW *might be needed for furling a square sail.*

DIE GANZE BESATZUNG *könnte nötig sein, um ein Rahsegel zu hissen.*

L'EQUIPE AU COMPLET *peut être nécessaire pour ferler une voile carrée.*

Un extrait du livre « Through Mighty Seas » par l'écrivain Henry Hughes, évoquant sa rencontre avec le marin John Davies.

La vie à bord était pleine de contrastes; d'un côté il y avait le travail acharné et le manque de sommeil, et de l'autre il y avait les couchers de soleils magnifiques, la douce brise des alizés, et les chansons de marin accompagnées à l'accordéon.

En 1905, l'Australien Jack McLaren à l'âge de dix-sept ans a été engagé à bord d'un trois-mâts en Australie.

Dans son livre dont le titre est révélateur « Blood on the Deck » (1933), il décrit la vie effroyable à bord, mais aussi les moments inoubliables :

« Parfois je me trouvais en haut du mât au lever du jour lorsque les premiers rayons de soleil commençaient à filtrer, esquissant un dessin sur l'eau et ensuite éclairant le haut des mâts avec un mélange d'or et d'argent. Le soleil brillait directement sur moi, comme s'il voulait examiner les traits de mon visage.

Le fait de naviguer sans moteur, utilisant la force puissante et naturelle du vent était une source de fierté et une grande satisfaction. »

C'est ainsi qu'un membre de l'équipage ou un passager à bord d'un Star Clippers peut décrire un lever du soleil, pendant que le bateau est en route des Canaries aux Caraïbes.

A bord, l'équipage est divisé en deux quarts - le quart tribord et le quart bâbord. Chaque quart travaille quatre heures et se repose ensuite quatre heures. Un système encore répandu sur de nombreux bateaux.

La cloche du bateau était utilisée pour indiquer le temps. L'officier frappait la cloche chaque demi-heure. Ainsi, après quatre heures, huit coups de cloche étaient donnés et il est temps de changer de quart. Afin d'éviter que les mêmes hommes prennent le même quart chaque jour, le quart entre 4 heures de l'après-midi et 8 heures était coupé en deux, connu comme le premier et le dernier petit quart. Ceux qui retournaient à leur quart à 4 heures, travaillaient seulement jusqu'à 6 heures et étaient libres jusqu' à 8 heures, et puis recommençaient à travailler.

Les équipages des clippers comptaient toujours de nombreuses nationalités et un mélange de marins expérimentés et de mousses, recrutés dans les bars des ports.

L' historien américain de la marine Arthur H Clark, écrit quelques lignes sur les marins:

« Parler de bienveillance et de mansuétude avec de tels hommes était une perte de temps, autant proposer un jardin d'enfants à des bébés coyotes ou des serpents à sonnette ». Il continua:

« Il y avait des Irlandais trapus et durs à cuire, leurs membres grossièrement tatoués; les Américains sur la route de la Californie était de la même espèce, coriaces et difficiles à discipliner à tel point que parfois il était difficile de savoir qui du capitaine ou des marins contrôlaient le navire.

Il y avait également des Espagnols, des Portugais, des Chinois, des Français, des Africains, des Russes et des Italiens. Certains venaient de la marine marchande et étaient d'excellents marins, d'autres par contre n'avaient rien à faire sur un bateau. »

Les seuls qui avaient une réelle expérience aux yeux de Clark, étaient les Scandinaves:

« D'excellents marins, propres, de bonne volonté, et obéissants, ils étaient les meilleurs et les premières classes d'hommes composant les équipages des clippers. »

Pour un jeune garçon, la vie de marin, dure et dangereuse, dans un environnement coriace, était difficile.

Robert Ramsay avait douze ans quand il signa son engagement sur un clipper en 1866. Dans le livre «Rough and Tumble on Old Clipper Ships», il décrit la façon dont il a été battu par un officier, de nombreuses fois pendant le voyage de Melbourne. L'officier utilisait un cordage, « mais il n'a jamais réussi à me faire pleurer. »

L'auteur danois de renommée internationale Carsten Jensen résume la vie à bord des clippers: « De nos jours, seuls les soldats au combats ont une vie comparable à celle des marins du 19e siècle. »

MANHOOD TEST in calm weather on the four-masted barque Hougomont, 1929.

MUTPROBE bei ruhigem Wetter auf der Viermastbark Hougomont im Jahre 1929.

TEST POUR DEVENIR un homme dur par temps calme sur le quatre-mâts barque. Hougomont, 1929.

OILSKINS AND SEA BISCUITS

In our dreams, we go back 150 years and stand on the deck of a clipper in the Southern Ocean. However, the dream might rather be a nightmare. What would feel most unfamiliar, most unbearable? The watch system? Hardly. That is something you get used to, as is witnessed by all the couples who have sailed a small boat across the oceans.

Working with the sail high up in the rigging? Hardly. If you are careless, it is deadly dangerous, but you get used to it, as long as you are not pathologically afraid of heights. The stench in the fo'c'sle of sweat, dirt, mould and bad tobacco? Hardly. The fresh air on deck compensates.

But the dampness and the food would be the hardest to endure. Continually wearing damp clothes and month after month having to shovel down the miserable food must be the worst.

The oilskins of the old days had nothing in common with today's trendy yachting clothes. They were coats and trousers made of canvas or course linen cloth. For waterproofing, they were soaked in linseed oil. When the oil had dried, which would take weeks, the fabric was miserably stiff and moderately water-repelling, at least to start with. But the salt water would soon penetrate, the clothes beneath would get moist and, because of the salt, they would never really dry.

As a result, salt water boils would develop. In the book "Leaves from a Sailor's Diary", J.M. Jardin describes a voyage in 1881, when everyone was tormented by salt water boils. Hardened sailors cried from pain, when the oilskins rubbed the boils. And everything was wet and sticky: bunks, blankets and clothes.

And then there was the food. It mainly consisted of heavily salted beef and pork of the worst quality, stored in barrels. It was accompanied by sea biscuits, most often infested with maggots. In the book Through Mighty Seas, Henry Hughes relates his first encounter with the maggots:

"Breaking the biscuit into convenient portions for eating, these brown-headed little devils met one's gaze. To the first voyager it was a revolting sight. They were not a bit shy, they would just remain there and squirm. The old salt would take little heed - he would dislodge the tenants by gently tapping the biscuit on the table, and then go on with the meal."

Wir träumen uns um 150 Jahre zurück und stehen auf dem Deck eines Klippers im südlichen Ozean. Der Traum ist aber vielleicht mehr ein Albtraum. Was würde sich am ungewohntesten, am unerträglichsten anfühlen?

Das Wachsystem? Kaum. Daran gewöhnt man sich; das wissen z. B. alle Paare, die ein kleines Boot über die Ozeane gesegelt haben. Mit den Segeln zu arbeiten hoch in der Takelage? Kaum. Es ist lebensgefährlich für den Unvorsichtigen, aber es wird zur Gewohnheit für den, der nicht krankhafte Höhenangst hat. Der Gestank von Schweiß, Schmutz, Schimmel und schlechtem Tabak im Mannschaftsraum? Kaum. Die frische Luft auf Deck gleicht das aus.

Aber die Nässe und das Essen waren am schwersten zu ertragen. Ständig feuchte Kleidung zu tragen und Monat für Monat die schlechte Verpflegung essen zu müssen, muss wohl das Schlimmste gewesen sein. Das Ölzeug der früheren Zeiten hatte nichts mit der modischen Sportkleidung von heute zu tun. Jacken und

---

OILSKIN was impregnated with linseed oil.

ÖLZEUG wurde mit Leinöl imprägniert.

LA TOILE CIREE était imprégnée d'huile de lin.

MENU 1890

Monday Breakfast: Coffee. Biscuits. Butter or marmalade. Dinner: Pea soup. Boiled salt pork. Biscuits. Tea: Milkless tea and biscuits.
Tuesday Breakfast: As on Monday. Dinner: Boiled salt beef and doughboys. Plum-duff. Biscuits. Tea: As on Monday.

Wednesday-Thursday As on Monday.
Friday As on Monday but stock fish instead of pork.
Saturday As on Monday.
Sunday Breakfast: As on Monday. Dinner: Boiled mutton tinned. Boiled rice. Biscuits. Tea: As on Monday.

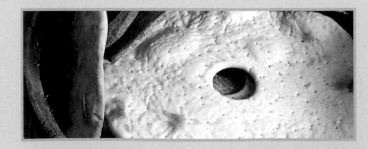

Hosen wurden aus Segeltuch oder grobem Leinen hergestellt. Diese wurden imprägniert, indem man sie in Leinöl tauchte. Wenn das Öl trocknete, und das dauerte Wochen, wurde das Tuch steif, war aber nur für den Anfang wasserabweisend.

Die Folge davon waren Salzwassergeschwüre. J.M. Jardin beschreibt in dem Buch „Leaves from a sailor's diary" eine Fahrt im Jahre 1881, bei der alle von Salzwassergeschwüren geplagt wurden. Harte Seeleute schrien vor Schmerz, wenn das Ölzeug auf den Geschwüren scheuerte. Alles war nass und klebrig: Kojen, Decken und Kleidung.

Und dann das Essen. Es bestand hauptsächlich aus hartem gesalzenem Rindfleisch und Schweinefleisch der übelsten Qualität, das in Tonnen verwahrt wurde. Dazu gab es Schiffszwieback, der sehr oft von Würmern wimmelte. Henry Hughes berichtet in dem Buch „Through Mighty Seas" über seine erste Erfahrung mit den Würmern:

„Brach man den Zwieback zum Essen in kleinere Teile, sah man plötzlich die kleinen Tierchen. Für den Neuling war es ein revoltierender Anblick. Sie waren überhaupt nicht scheu, sie blieben einfach da und wanden sich. Der alte Seebär dagegen, machte sich nichts daraus; er entfernte die Bewohner, indem er den Zwieback leicht an den Tisch klopfte und dann mit seiner Mahlzeit fortfuhr."

Et si l'on faisait un petit saut en arrière de 150 ans pour se trouver à bord d'un clipper au beau milieu de l'océan du sud; serait-ce un rêve ou un cauchemar? Qu'est ce qui serait le plus difficile à supporter? Les Quarts? Absolument pas, selon les témoignages de ceux qui ont traversé les océans à bord d'un petit bateau on s'y habitue très facilement.

Travailler en haut du mât avec les voiles?

A peine. Si vous ne faites pas attention, c'est très dangereux, mais vous vous y habituez, tant que vous n'avez pas le vertige.

L'odeur infecte de la sueur dans le poste de l'équipage, de la saleté, de la moisissure et du mauvais tabac? A peine. L'air frais sur le pont compense.

Mais l'humidité et la nourriture étaient le plus dur à vivre. Porter continuellement des vêtements mouillés mois après mois, manger misérablement étaient le pire.

Les toiles cirées du vieux temps n'ont rien à voir avec les vêtements modernes pour la voile d'aujourd'hui. C'étaient des vestes et des pantalons en toile de lin. Pour les rendre étanches, ils étaient trempés dans de l'huile de lin. Quand l'huile avait séché, ce qui pouvait prendre des semaines, le résultat était complètement raide, peu imperméable ce qui entraînait des infections au contact de l'eau salée. " Il y avait la nourriture qui consistait principalement en du boeuf fortement salé et du porc de mauvaise qualité, stockée dans des tonneaux et accompagnée de biscuits à l'eau de mer, le plus souvent infectée d'asticots.

« C'est en cassant le biscuit en petites portions que les petites bêtes aux yeux noirs attiraient votre regard. Au premier voyage c'était une vision horrible! Ce n'était pas du tout une question de timidité, elles restaient là en se tortillant. Le vieux loup de mer y attachait peu d'importance. Il tapotait doucement son biscuit pour en faire partir les « visiteurs » et continuait tranquillement son repas. »

(Henry Hughs - Through Mighty Seas)

MENUE 1890

Montag Frühstück: Kaffee, Zwieback, Butter oder Marmelade, Abendessen: Erbsensuppe, Gekochtes Schweinefleisch, Zwieback. Tee ohne Milch und Zwieback.
Dienstag Frühstück: Wie am Montag Abendessen: Gekochtes Rindfleisch und Gebackenes, Pudding, Zwieback.

Mittwoch und Donnerstag Wie am Montag.
Freitag Wie am Montag aber getrockneter Fisch.
Samstag Wie am Montag.
Sonntag Frühstück: Wie am Montag, Abendessen: Gekochter Hammel, gekochter Reis, Zwieback.

MENU 1890

Lundi Petit déjeuner. Café. Biscuits. Beurre ou marmelade. Dîner: soupe de pois cassés. Porc salé bouilli. Biscuits, thé sans lait et biscuits.
Mardi Petit déjeuner. Comme lundi. Diner: boeuf salé bouilli. Pudding à la prune. Biscuits. Thé: comme lundi.

Mercredi et jeudi Comme lundi.
Vendredi Comme lundi mais du merluche à la place du porc.
Samedi Comme lundi.
Dimanche Petit déjeuner: comme lundi. Diner: mouton bouilli en boîte. Riz bouilli. Biscuits. Thé: comme lundi.

A BEER for the ship's pig

DAS SCHIFFSSCHWEIN bekommt ein Bier

UNE BIERE pour le cochon du bord.

SUN, STARS AND SOME LUCK

s it possible to find one's way across the ocean without navigational instruments? Without compass. Without sextant. Without log. And of course without modern satellite navigation. Obviously. In 1982, Marvin Creamer, 67 and Professor of Geography from New Jersey, sailed around the world without navigational instruments or timekeeper.

His small boat, *Globe Star*, was only 36 feet (11 metres) and the voyage took one and a half years, of which seven months were at sea. Sun, moon, stars, wave formations, colour of water and birds were the only aids.

Others have done the same, but only for shorter distances.

The magnetic compass was known in China two thousand years ago. In Europe, it was first used in Italian ships in the 12th century.

In the Middle Ages, astronomical instruments for measuring latitude were developed: astrolabe, Davis quadrant, Jacob's staff and later the more exact instruments octant and sextant - sextant, since the scale of a sextant has a length of 1/6 turn (60°). What is measured is the angle between the sea horizon and the sun. It is then possible to calculate the latitude.

But in order to calculate the position of the ship, you also need to know your longitude. That requires a very reliable clock - a chronometer. A clock that could withstand the movements in a ship and show the right time to the second during month-long ocean voyages did not exist until 1730. The first such clock was built by the English carpenter and clock maker John Harrison.

At sea, compass, sextant and chronometer were the most important navigational instruments up to the 1970's.

THE MATE taking the altitude of the sun and the Greenwich Observatory.

DER STEUERMANN misst die Sonnenhöhe mit dem Sextanten, und das Observatorium in Greenwhich

L'OFFICIER mesure la hauteur du soleil, et l'Observatoire de Greenwich.

THE PRIME MERIDIAN

Since 1884, the prime meridian passes through Greenwich, London. It is the reference for charts and for time measurement all over the world. The prime meridian divides the earth into a western and an eastern hemisphere. But before 1884, there were some thirty different prime meridians. One passed through the White House in Washington, one through the old Paris observatory etc. The exact position has been slightly adjusted. It is now 336 feet east of the famous Greenwich tourist attraction. On that spot, you will find a waste-paper bin!

Kann man sich auf dem Meer ohne Navigationshilfen zurechtfinden? Ohne Kompass, ohne Sextant und natürlich ohne moderne Navigation mit Satelliten. Offensichtlich. 1982 segelte Martin Creamer, 67 Jahre alt und Professor der Geographie von New Jersey rund um die Erde ohne Uhr und Navigationsinstrumente. Sein kleines Boot *Globe Star* war nur 36 Fuß lang und die Reise dauerte achtzehn Monate, davon sieben auf See.

Es war Navigation durch Wahrnehmungen. Sonne, Mond, Sterne, Wellenform, Farbe des Wassers und Vögel waren die einzigen Hilfsmittel.

Der Magnetkompass war in China seit 2000 Jahren bekannt. In Europa wurde er zuerst auf italienischen Schiffen im 12. Jahrhundert angewendet. Im Mittelalter entwickelte man astronomische Instrumente, um die Breitengrade zu bestimmen: Astrolabium, Davids Quadrant, Jakobs Stab und später die viel genaueren Geräte wie Oktant und Sextant. Der Name Sextant ergab sich, weil er eine Skala von 60 Grad hat (1/6stel eines Kreises). Man misst den Winkel zwischen dem Meereshorizont und der Sonne. Daraus kann man den Breitengrad berechnen.

Um aber die genaue Position des Schiffes zu berechnen, muss man auch den Längengrad kennen; dazu benötigt man eine sehr zuverlässige Uhr - einen Chronometer. Eine Uhr, die die Schiffsbewegungen vertragen konnte und die die richtige Zeit auch nach monatelanger Seereise bis auf die Sekunde genau anzeigte, gab es nicht vor 1730.

Die erste wurde von dem englischen Tischler und Uhrmacher John Harrison hergestellt. Zur See waren der Kompass, der Sextant und der Chronometer die wichtigsten Navigationsinstrumente bis in die Mitte der 70iger Jahre.

Est-il possible de trouver un moyen pour traverser l'océan sans instrument de navigation ? Sans boussole, sans sextant et sans log. Et bien sûr sans instrument moderne de navigation par satellite. Apparemment oui. En 1982, Morvin Creamer, 67 ans et professeur de géographie, du New Jersey, navigue autour du monde sans instrument de navigation ou d'horloge.

Son petit bateau, le *Globe Star*, de seulement 36 pieds de long (11 mètres) fit le voyage en un an et demi, dont sept mois en mer. Grâce au soleil, à la lune, aux étoiles, à la formation des vagues, la couleur de l'eau et les oiseaux.

La boussole était connue en Chine il y a deux mille ans. En Europe, elle a été utilisée pour la première fois par des bateaux italiens au 12ème siècle. Au Moyen Age, des instruments astronomiques pour mesurer la latitude existaient déjà: l'astrolabe, le cadran de Devis, le bâton de Jacob et plus tard des instruments plus exacts comme l'octant et le sextant. On a donné à cet instrument le nom de sextant car son arc gradué est du sixième de la circonférence. Il permet donc de mesurer l'angle entre l' horizon sur l'eau et le soleil afin de déterminer la latitude.

Mais pour calculer la position du bateau, vous avez aussi besoin de connaître la longitude. Cela nécessite d'avoir une horloge fiable - un chronomètre. Une horloge qui peut supporter les mouvements d'un bateau et donner l'heure exacte à la seconde près pendant les longs mois des voyages océaniques. Une telle horloge a été construite, la première fois par un charpentier et horloger anglais John Harrison en 1730. En mer, la boussole, le sextant et le chronomètre étaient les instruments de navigation les plus importants jusqu'aux années 1970.

DER NULL MERIDIAN

Seit 1884 geht der Nullmeridian durch Greenwich, London. Er ist der Ausgangspunkt für Seekarten und die Zeitmessung über die ganze Welt. Der Nullmeridian teilt die Welt in eine westliche und eine östliche Hälfte. Vor 1884 gab es an die dreißig verschiedenen Nullmeridiane. Einer ging durch die Church of the Holy Sepulchre in Jerusalem, einer durch das Observatorium in Paris usw. Der genaue Verlauf ist heute etwas korrigiert worden. Er liegt 102,5 Meter östlich der Sehenswürdigkeit in Greenwich. An der Stelle steht ein Papierkorb!

LE PREMIER MERIDIEN

Depuis 1884, le premier méridien passe à travers Greenwich à Londres. C'est la référence pour les cartes et pour la mesure du temps dans le monde entier. Le premier méridien divise la terre en hémisphère ouest et est. Avant 1884, il y avait quelques trente différents premiers méridiens. Il y en a un qui passe à travers le vieil observatoire de Paris et un à travers l'église du Saint Sépulture de Holy à Jérusalem etc. La position exacte a été légèrement ajustée. Elle se situe maintenant à 102,5 mètres à l'est du fameux site touristique. A cet endroit, vous trouverez une poubelle!

JACOB'S STAFF, a mediaeval predecessor of the sextant.

JAKOBSTAB, Vorgänger des Sextanten im Mittelalter

UNE MIRE DE JACOB, un instrument médiéval du sextant.

WEIRD WORDS

CL RL EGNS APA APS BOD
BWC ARPA BWR BRG CPA
GPS HDG CMG COG CTS XTE
DOP MOB DTK DTS DST
DCPA EBL ETE ETA GC HDG
LKP LAT LNG MRK POS
RNG RBL RL RTE SHM SOG
SOW TCPA TTG TZ TRK UTC
VRM WPT VMG WGS YDS

Could anyone please tell me who is firing and what he is firing at." Today, the question put by the British admiral Jellicoe during the Battle of Jutland in 1916 seems somewhat bizarre. His flagship, HMS *Iron Duke*, was rushing at twenty knots towards the German fleet.

But it was foggy, and neither Admiral Jellicoe nor the look-outs in the crow's nest could see anything ahead.

Up until the mid-20th century the capacity to establish the movement and position of other ships was somewhat limited. Good visibility was a prerequisite.

During World War II, various navigational aids were developed, such as radar, Decca and Loran. Radar uses reflecting high-frequency radio beams. Decca and Loran use low-frequency radio beams that are transmitted from several fixed radio beacons.

In the 1970s, the Americans developed the GPS (Global Positioning System). It is based on signals from satellites (today more than 20). In May, 1994, commercial shipping, pleasure craft and airplanes got access to the signals, which had previously been coded.

GPS makes it possible to obtain an exact position (longitude, latitude and altitude) anywhere on the globe. It can be combined with an electronic chart. On the screen, the position of one's ship is marked directly on the chart. Radar and other electronic systems can complement the picture, making the position, speed and course of other ships visible on the screen. The weakest link today is the charts, which rarely are as exact as the GPS.

Könnte mir bitte jemand sagen, wer feuert und auf was er feuert." Eine heutzutage grotesk anmutende Frage des britischen Admirals Jellicoe während der Skagerrakschlacht im Jahre 1916. Zur selben Zeit dampfte sein Flaggschiff HMS *Iron Duke* mit zwanzig Knoten auf die deutsche Flotte zu. Es war Nebel und Admiral Jellicoe sah nichts weiter, als was seine Posten in den Ausgucks berichten konnten.

Die Möglichkeit, die eigene Position zu bestimmen und die Bewegungen anderer Schiffe zu verfolgen, war bis zur Mitte des 20. Jahrhunderts begrenzt. Gute Sicht war Voraussetzung.

Während des 2. Weltkrieges wurden verschiedene Navigationshilfen entwickelt, hyperbelnavigation unter anderem Radar, Decca und Loran. Radar verwendet reflektierende Hochfrequenz-Radiowellen. Decca und Loran benutzen Niedrigfrequenz Radiowellen, die von mehreren feststehenden Radiostationen ausgesandt werden.

In den siebziger Jahren des letzten Jahrhunderts entwickelten die Amerikaner das GPS System (Global Positioning System). Es stützt sich auf Signale von Satelliten (heute gut 20 Stück). Im Mai 1994 erhielten die Berufsschifffahrt, private Boote und Flugzeuge, Zugang zu den bis dahin verschlüsselten Signalen.

Mit GPS kann man eine exakte Position für Länge, Breite und Höhe an jeder Stelle der Erde bestimmen. GPS kann auch mit einer elektronischen Seekarte kombiniert werden. Auf dem Bildschirm erscheint dann die Position des eigenen Schiffes direkt auf der Seekarte.

Zusätzlich können Radar und andere elektronische Systeme das Bild komplettieren. So erscheinen z.B. die Position anderer Schiffe, ihre Geschwindigkeit und der Kurs auf dem Bildschirm. Die größte Fehlerquelle sind heutzutage die Seekarten, die selten dieselbe Genauigkeit wie GPS haben.

S'il vous plait, quelqu'un peut-il me dire qui tire et qu'elle est la cible? » Aujourd'hui, la question posée par l'amiral anglais Jellicoe pendant la Bataille de Jutland en 1916 semble quelque peu bizarre. Son navire amiral, le HMS *Iron Duke*, se ruait à vingt nœuds vers la flotte Allemande. Mais il y avait du brouillard, et ni l'amiral Jellicoe ni les matelots dans la sentinelle ne pouvaient voir quoi que ce soit.

La possibilité d'établir la position et le déplacement des autres bateaux était limité jusqu'au milieu du 20ème siècle. Une bonne visibilité était indispensable. Pendant la deuxième Guerre Mondiale, diverses aides à la navigation ont été développées, comme le radar, le Decca et le Loran. Le radar utilise la réflexion des ondes de haute fréquence qui sont transmises par plusieurs radios phares

fixés. Dans les années 1970, les Américains ont développé le GPS (Global Positionning System). Il est basé sur l'émission venant de satellites (aujourd'hui il y en existe plus de 20).

En mai 1994, la navigation commerciale et de plaisance ainsi que l'aviation accédèrent à des signaux jusqu'alors codés. Le GPS permet d'obtenir une position exacte (longitude, latitude et altitude) n'importe où sur le globe.

Il peut être combiné avec une carte électronique. Sur l'écran, la position d'un bateau est indiquée directement sur la carte. Le radar et d'autres systèmes électroniques peuvent compléter l'ensemble, afin d'obtenir la position, la vitesse et le cheminement des autres bateaux visibles sur l'écran. Le maillon le plus faible aujourd'hui reste les cartes, qui sont rarement aussi exactes que le GPS.

THE GPS, Global Positioning System is based on signals from satellites. Today more than 20.

DAS GPS - Global Positioning System. stützt sich auf Signale von Satelliten. Heute gut 20 Stück.

LE GPS - Global Positioning System. Basé sur l'émission venant de satellites. Aujourd'hui il y en a plus de 20.

MOB
Man Over Board

ETA
Estimated Time of Arrival

COG
Course Over Ground

SOG
Speed Over Ground

TTG
Time To Go

UTC
Coordinated Universal Time

TWIST AND SHOUT

Muscles and teamwork were the necessary prerequisites for weighing the anchor, hoisting the sails and working the pump for hours and hours. Such tasks could be made easier by rhythmic singing. The shanties were the special working songs of the sailors.

A shantyman, maybe with an accordion or a fiddle, would sing the lyrics and the crewmen, pulling the rope or walking the capstan, would respond with the refrain. "Away-aye, blow the man down!" Different tasks required different paces of work. The pump one pace. The capstan another, braces and sheets a third. That was why there were different shanties for different work.

A skilled shantyman would also be able to improvise his own words to a well known melody, words that could tell a joke about the officers. Most of the shanties are in English, but there are also shanties in German and French.

There was also another musical tradition on board ship. On calm days, instruments would be taken out in the free watch. A guitar, an accordion or a mouth organ. There would be singing, maybe even dancing on deck. But it was sea songs, not shanties, that were sung, popular tunes in 3/4 time, a rare beat in shanties, since it is difficult to work to.

Muskelkraft und Zusammenarbeit waren notwendig, wenn der Anker gelichtet werden sollte, wenn die Segel gehisst und die Pumpen für Stunden in Betrieb gehalten werden mussten Da erleichtert ein taktfester Gesang die Arbeit. Die Shanties waren spezielle Arbeitslieder der Seeleute.

Ein Vorsänger, ein Shantymann, vielleicht mit einer Ziehharmonika oder Geige, sang den Text und die Seeleute, die einholten oder an dem Gangspill gingen, sangen im Kehrreim. „Away-aye, blow the man down!" Unterschiedliche Arbeiten erforderten unterschiedliche Arbeitstakte. Die Pumpe hatte einen Takt, das Gangspill einen anderen, Brassen und Schoten einen dritten.

Daher gab es unterschiedliche Shanties für verschiedene Arbeitsaufgaben. Ein geschickter

Shantymann konnte auch eigene Texte mit einer bekannten Melodie improvisieren. Solche Texte konnten sich über die Schiffsführung lustig machen. Die meisten Shanties sind englisch, es gibt sie aber auch auf deutsch und französisch.

Es gab auch eine weitere Musiktradition an Bord. An ruhigen Tagen holte man während der Freiwache Instrumente hervor. Eine Gitarre, eine Geige, eine Ziehharmonika, eine Mundharmonika. Aber jetzt sang man nicht Shanties sondern Seemannslieder, populäre Weisen im Dreiviertel takt. Dieser wurde selten bei einem Shanty angewendet - es ist schwer danach zu arbeiten.

Des hommes musclés et du travail d'équipe étaient nécessaires pour remonter l'ancre, hisser les voiles et pomper pendant des heures et des heures. Des tâches difficiles rendues moins pénibles par les chants rythmés.

Les chants étaient spécifiques au travail des marins. Un chanteur, parfois avec un accordéon ou un violon, improvisait des paroles et l'équipage, tirant sur les cordages, marchant ou faisant fonctionner le cabestan, pouvait répondre avec le refrain: « Away-aye, souffle sur l'homme! »

Chaque chanson correspondait à une tâche spécifique; il y avait des chansons pour hisser, des chansons pour virer et des chansons pour ramer etc.

Un chanteur expérimenté était même capable d'improviser et mettre de nouvelles paroles sur une mélodie traditionnelle y ajoutant quelques blagues à propos des officiers par exemple.

La plupart des chansons étaient en Anglais, mais il y a aussi des chansons en Allemand et en Français.

Il y avait également d'autres traditions musicales à bord; par temps calme, lorsque les marins étaient au repos, ils chantaient et dansaient ensemble accompagnés d'un harmonica ou d'une guitare. C'étaient des mélodies populaires écrites sur une mesure 3/4, ce qui les différenciait des chants de travail car il est très difficile de travailler sur un tel rythme.

ROLLING HOME

Up aloft, amid the rigging
Swiftly blows the fav'ring gale,
Strong as springtime in its blossom,
Filling out each bending sail,
And the waves we leave behind us
Seem to murmur as they rise;
We have tarried here to bear you
To the land you dearly prize.

Rolling home, rolling home,
Rolling home across the sea,
Rolling home to dear old England
Rolling home, dear land to thee.

Now, it takes all hands to man the capstan,
Mister see your cables clear!
Soon you'll be sailing homeward bound sir,
And for the channel you will steer.
See your sheets and clew lines free sir,
All your buntlines overhauled;
Are the sheerpoles and gear all ready?
Soon for New England we will steer.

Rolling home, rolling home,
Rolling home across the sea,
Rolling home to dear old England
Rolling home, dear land to thee.

Full ten thousand miles behind us,
And a thousand miles before,
Ancient ocean waves to waft us
To the well remembered shore.
Newborn breezes swell to send us
To our childhood welcome skies,
To the glow of friendly faces
And the glance of loving eyes.

Rolling home, rolling home,
Rolling home across the sea,
Rolling home to dear old England
Rolling home, dear land to thee.

Charles MacMay 1858?

MEERESSTILLE

Tiefe Stille herrscht im Wasser,
Ohne Regung ruht das Meer,
Und bekümmert sieht der Schiffer
Glatte Fläche ringsumher.
Keine Luft von keiner Seite!
Todesstille fürchterlich!
In der ungeheuern Weite
Reget keine Welle sich.

Johann Wolfgang von Goethe „Glückliche Fahrt" 1795

Now, it takes all hands to man the capstan

L´HOMME ET LA MER

Homme libre, toujours tu chériras la mer!
La mer est ton miroir; tu contemples ton âme
Dans le déroulement infini de sa lame,
Et ton esprit n'est pas un gouffre moins amer.

Tu te plais à plonger au sein de ton image;
Tu l'embrasses des yeux et des bras, et ton coeur
Se distrait quelquefois de sa propre rumeur
Au bruit de cette plainte indomptable et sauvage.

Vous êtes tous les deux ténébreux et discrets,
Homme, nul n'a sondé le fond de tes abîmes;
O mer, nul ne connaît tes richesses intimes,
Tant vous êtes jaloux de garder vos secrets!

Et cependant voilà des siècles innombrables
Que vous vous combattez sans pitié ni remord,
Tellement vous aimez le carnage et la mort,
O lutteurs éternels, ô frères implacables!

Charles Baudelaire "Les Fleurs Du Mal" 1857

SLOOP JOHN B.

We come on the sloop John B
My grandfather and me
Around Nassau town we did roam.
Drinking all night. Got into a fight.
Well I feel so broke up, I want to go home

So hoist up the John B's sail
See how the mainsail sets
Call for the captain ashore. Let me go home.
Let me go home, I wanna go home, yeah yeah
Well I feel so broke up I wanna go home.

The poor cook he caught the fits
And threw away all my grits
And then he took and he ate up all of my corn.
Let me go home, why don't they let me go home,
This is the worst trip, I've ever been on.

Traditional

SEA-FEVER

I must go down to the seas again,
to the lonely sea and the sky,
And all I ask is a tall ship
and a star to steer her by,
And the wheel's kick and the wind's song
and the white sail's shaking,
And a grey mist on the sea's face,
and a grey dawn breaking.

John Masefield "Salt-Water Ballads" 1902

WHAT SHALL WE DO WITH THE DRUNKEN SAILOR

What shall we do with the drunken sailor,
What shall we do with the drunken sailor,
What shall we do with the drunken sailor ,
Earlye in the morning.

Chorus:
Hooray and up she rises,
Hooray and up she rises,
Hooray and up she rises,
Earlye in the morning.

Put him in the long boat till he's sober,
Put him in the long boat till he's sober,
Put him in the long boat till he's sober,
Earlye in the morning
Chorus: Hooray...

Pull out the plug and wet him all over,
Pull out the plug and wet him all over,
Pull out the plug and wet him all over,
Earley in the morning.
Chorus: Hooray...

Heave him by the leg in a running bowlin',
Heave him by the leg in a running bowlin',
Heave him by the leg in a running bowlin',
Earlye in the morning
Chorus: Hooray...

Shanty

BLOW THE MAN DOWN
Come all you young fellows that follow the sea
To my way, ay, blow the man down
And pray pay attention and listen to me.
Oh, give me some time to blow the man down!

As I was walking down Paradise Street
Way! Hey! Blow the man down!
A pretty young damsel I happened to meet.
She had a man, oh, blow the man down!

I hailed her in English, she answered me clear:
Way! Hey! Blow the man down!
I took the suggestion and I had no fear.
Give me some time to blow the man down!

I swung to the left and I swung to the right.
Way! Hey! Blow the man down!
But he was a guy who sure knew how to fight.
Give me some time to blow the man down!

Guess I had one too many with pals at the bar.
Way! Hey! Blow the man down!
Or else I'd be certain to lick him by far.
Give me som time to blow the man down!

The adorable damsel, when she saw me fall
Way! Hey! Blow the man down!
Took off with her hero so handsome and tall.
Give me some time to blow the man down!

All ye sailors take warning before you set sail.
Way! Hey! Blow the man down!
If he's strong as an ox and big as a whale
Think twice before you blow the man down!

Shanty

Shipshape

and Bristol Fashion

THERE ARE HAPPY SHIPS and unhappy ships. An old salt knows the difference before he goes on board. It has to do with orderliness, but also with matching ship type and trade.

ES GIBT GLÜCKLICHE SCHIFFE und unglückliche Schiffe. Ein alter Seebär erkennt den Unterschied bevor er an Bord geht. Es geht um Ordnung, aber auch um die Abstimmung von Schiffstyp und Reiseroute.

IL Y A DES BATEAUX HEUREUX et des bateaux malheureux. Un vieux loup de mer connaît la différence avant de monter à bord. Cela relève de discipline, mais aussi du type de bateau et du type de commerce.

KNOTS YOU SHOULD KNOW

There are about 4,000 different knots. A fisherman will use special knots in tying his nets, a florist in creating bouquets, a horseman in harnessing his horse, a seamstress in embroidering, an artist in decorating and the hangman in slipping the noose around the neck of the condemned.

The miles of rope that form the rigging of a sailing vessel demand many different knots, splices and seizings. A knot should have the following properties:

It must hold. It should cause as little wear as possible on the rope. It must be easy to tie. It must be easy to untie. It should preferably look beautiful and harmonious.

No civilisation is possible without ropes and knots. Stone Age axe makers revolutionised their trade by tying the blade to the handle with sinews or osiers.

The door of Tutankhamen's tomb was lashed with a rope. It was 3,000 years old, but looked surprisingly modern. And a 15,000 year old cave painting in Spain depicts a rope.

There are six different knots, which are equally useful at sea and ashore.

1. Reef knot - used for joining two ropes of equal thickness. 2. Figure of eight knot - used for making a knob at the end of a rope. 3. Clove hitch - used for mooring small craft. 4. Two half hitches - used for securing a line to a ring. 5. Bowline - forms a loop at the end of a rope. 6. Carrick bend - used for joining two ropes of different thickness.

And what about the best known of all knots, the Gordian knot which nobody could untie, until Alexander the Great parted it with his sword. It was probably some kind of stopper, possibly a Monkey's Fist.

Es gibt 4 000 unterschiedliche Knoten. Ein Fischer wendet spezielle Knoten an, wenn er seine Netze knüpft, ein Florist, wenn er seine Blumensträuße bindet, ein Reiter, wenn er sein Pferd sattelt, eine Schneiderin, wenn sie stickt, ein Künstler, wenn er dekoriert und der Henker, wenn er die Schlinge um den Hals des Todeskandidaten legt.

Die kilometerlangen Seile auf einem Segelschiff erfordern eine Menge verschiedener Knoten und Spleiße.

Ein Knoten sollte die folgenden Eigenschaften haben:

Er muss halten. Er sollte die Festigkeit des Seiles so wenig wie möglich beeinträchtigen. Er muss leicht zu knüpfen und leicht zu lösen sein. Er sollte möglichst gut und harmonisch aussehen. Keine Zivilisation kann ohne Seile und Knoten auskommen. Die Steinäxte, die man benutzte, waren mit geknoteten Sehnen zusammengefügt.

Die Tür zu Tutanchamuns Grabkammer war mit einem Seil gesichert. Es war 3 000 Jahre alt und sah verblüffend modern aus. Und auf einer 15 000 Jahre alten Höhlenmalerei in Spanien ist ein Seil abgebildet.

Sechs verschiedene Knoten sollte man kennen, die an Land und zur See gleich nützlich sind.

1. Kreuzknoten wird angewendet, um zwei Seile gleicher Stärke zu verbinden. 2. Achterknoten wird angewendet, um einen Knoten am Ende des Seils zu machen. 3. Webeleinstek wird zum Vertäuen kleinerer Boote benutzt. 4. Zwei Halbschläge benutzt man, um ein Seil an einem Ring zu befestigen. 5. Palstek bildet eine Schlinge am Ende des Seils. 6. Schotstek benutzt man, um zwei ungleich starke Seile mit einander zu verbinden.

Il y a environ 4 000 nœuds différents. Un pêcheur utilisera des nœuds spéciaux pour tendre ses filets, il en sera de même pour le fleuriste qui créé des bouquets, un cavalier qui harnache son cheval, une couturière pour la broderie, un artiste pour la décoration et un bourreau qui passe le nœud coulant autour du cou du condamné.

Les marins utilisent des kilomètres de cordage et différents types de nœuds pour le gréement des bateaux. Un nœud devra avoir les propriétés suivantes:

Il doit tenir. Il doit aussi causer aussi peu de dommages que possible au cordage. Il doit être facile à défaire. De préférence, il doit être beau et harmonieux.

Aucune civilisation n'a existé sans cordage et sans nœud. A l'âge de pierre la vie fût révolutionnée en fixant les pierres taillées avec des tendons ou de l'osier. La dalle de la tombe de Toutankhamon était fixée avec une corde. Cela s'est passé il y a 3 000 ans mais le noeud était très moderne. Une caverne peinte il y a 15 000 ans en Espagne montrait une corde.

Il y a six nœuds différents, qui sont couramment utilisés en mer et à terre:

1. Nœud plat utilisé pour joindre deux cordages de diamètres égaux. 2. Nœud de huit utilisé pour faire un bouton à l'extrémité d'un cordage.
3. Demi-clé (nœud de cabestan) utilisé pour amarrer un petit bateau. 4. Deux demi-clés utilisées pour sécuriser une amarre à une bite d'amarrage.
5. Nœud de chaise qui forme une boucle à l'extrémité d'un cordage. 6. Nœud d'écoute (nœud de Carrick) - utilisé pour attacher ensemble deux cordages de diamètres différents.

THE SEAMAN´S BIBLE

It has been called The Seaman's Bible, "The Ashley Book of Knots". This book of 620 pages describes 3,900 knots in 7,000 drawings. The first edition was published in 1944. The American Clifford W. Ashley had then been collecting material about knots for forty years.

"A knot is either exactly right or it is hopelessly wrong", was his slogan.

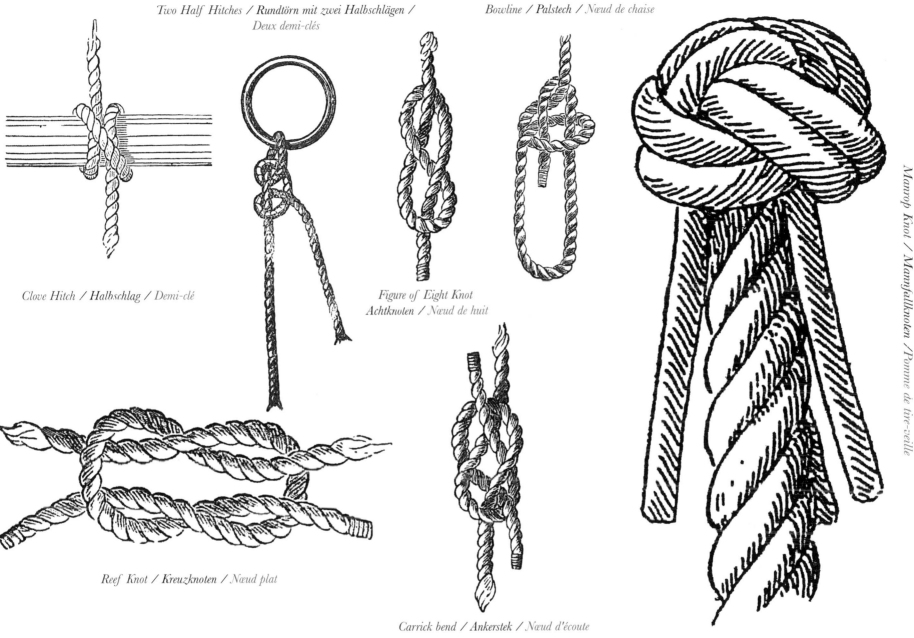

Two Half Hitches / Rundtörn mit zwei Halbschlägen / Deux demi-clés

Bowline / Palstech / Nœud de chaise

Clove Hitch / Halbschlag / Demi-clé

Figure of Eight Knot Achtknoten / Nœud de huit

Reef Knot / Kreuzknoten / Nœud plat

Carrick bend / Ankerstek / Nœud d'écoute

Manrop Knot / Mannfallknoten / Pomme de tire-veille

DIE BIBEL DES SEEMANNS

Man nennt sie allgemein die Bibel des Seemanns, „The Ashley Book of Knots". Das 620 Seiten starke Buch enthält 7 000 Zeichnungen und beschreibt über 3 900 Knoten. Die erste Auflage kam 1944 heraus. Zu dem Zeitpunkt hatte der Amerikaner Clifford W. Ashley über vierzig Jahre lang Material über verschiedene Knoten gesammelt. „Ein Knoten ist entweder genau richtig oder hoffnungslos falsch", war sein Sprichwort.

LA BIBLE DU MARIN

On appelait la Bible du marin, le livre des nœuds de Ashley. Ce livre de 620 pages décrit 3 900 nœuds en 7 000 dessins. La première édition parût en 1944. L'américain Clifford W. Ashley a rassemblé les informations sur les nœuds pendant quarante ans.

Sa devise était: « Un nœud est soit exactement correct, soit il est désespérément mauvais. »

SURVIVAL OF THE FITTEST

Sailors have a saying: "When you come to the end of the line, bend on another one". Life at sea was often a question of survival, just like Charles Darwin said in his theory of natural selection. "Survival of the fittest" can also be applied to ships and ship types. Incidentally, Darwin's On the Origin of Species was published in 1859, in the golden age of the clipper ships. If a ship is to be happy, she has to be built for the seas she is going to sail and the cargoes she is going to carry. That explains why boats and ships look so different. The wrong type of ship in the wrong waters means less profit for the owner or even worse - the ship may founder.

On the contrary, the right ship in the right waters may earn good revenue for the owner and happy voyages for the ship. The basic rule reads:

A ship that sails in trade winds and monsoons, where the wind direction is constant for months, should carry sails for following winds - large square sails. A ship that sails along the coast with both following winds and head winds should have fore-and-aft sails, like gaff sails. A gaff sail is more efficient in an adverse wind, when the ship has to beat to windward. This explains why there have been so many types of ships and rigs. The names have varied, even within the same culture and language, but these are the most common.

Seeleute haben ein Sprichwort: „Wenn Du an das Ende des Seils kommst, knüpfe ein anderes an." Das Leben an Bord war nicht selten eine Frage des Überlebens, so wie Charles Darwin es in seiner Theorie um die natürliche Auslese formulierte. „Survival of the Fittest" kann auch auf Schiffe und Schiffstypen angewendet werden. Wie durch Zufall wurde Darwins Buch „On the Origin of Species" (Über den Ursprung der Arten) im Jahre 1859 veröffentlicht, zu der Blütezeit der Klipperschiffe.

Wenn ein Schiff glücklich sein soll, muss es für die Gewässer gebaut sein, auf den es segeln soll, und für die Ladung, die es befördern soll. Daraus erklärt sich, warum Boote und Schiffe so unterschiedlich aussehen. Falscher Schiffstyp auf falsche See bedeutet weniger Gewinn für den Reeder oder schlimmer noch - Verlust des Schiffes. Als Gegenstück, das richtige Schiff auf der richtigen

See kann für den Reeder gute Geschäfte und glückliche Fahrten für das Schiff bedeuten. Hier sind die Grundregeln: Ein Schiff, das im Passat oder Monsun segelt, mit gleicher Windrichtung über Monate hinweg, sollte Segel haben, um vor dem Wind zu segeln, also große viereckige Rahsegel. Ein Schiff, das entlang der Küste, sowohl vor dem Wind, als auch am Wind segelt, sollte Gaffelsegel haben. Ein Gaffelsegel ist effektiver bei Gegenwind, wenn das Schiff kreuzen muss. Dies erklärt, warum es so viele unterschiedliche Schiffstypen und Takelungen gab. Die Namen waren auch innerhalb der gleichen Kultur und Sprache unterschiedlich, aber hier sind die gebräuchlichsten.

Les marins ont un dicton: « Quand vous vous approchez de la destination, recherchez en une autre. » La vie à bord était souvent une question de survie, tout juste comme le dit Charles Darwin dans sa théorie sur la sélection naturelle: « La sélection naturelle peut aussi être appliquée aux bateaux et aux autres types de bateaux. » Soit dit en passant, L'Origine des Espèces a été publiée en 1859, pendant l'âge d'or des clippers.

Si un bateau doit être heureux, il doit être construit pour les mers pour lesquelles il va naviguer, et adapté aux cargaisons qu'il aura à transporter. Cela explique pourquoi les bateaux ont des aspects si différents. Le mauvais type de bateau sur des eaux mauvaises veut dire moins de profit pour l'armateur et pire encore - le bateau pourrait sombrer. Au contraire, le bon bateau sur des eaux favorables peut être un bon revenu pour le propriétaire et une traversée heureuse pour le navire. La règle de base: Un bateau qui navigue avec les alizés et la mousson, là où la direction du vent est constante pendant des mois peut porter les voiles pour des vents portants – et des voiles de grande surface. Un bateau qui navigue le long des côtes avec aussi bien des vents portants que des vents contraires devrait avoir des voiles auriques et des voiles de flèche. Une voile de flèche est plus efficace par vent contraire quand le bateau doit lutter pour remonter au vent. Ceci explique pourquoi il y a tellement de bateaux et de gréements différents. Les appellations sont variées, mais ceci est le plus commun.

CLIPPER SHIP
Three masts, all carrying square sails. They were built for fast ocean passages - with golddiggers and goods from the US east coast to California, later also to Australia, or with tea and spices from China to England. The clippers had a protruding stem, and the maximum width of the hull was further astern than in comparable ships. The length was at least five times the width and the draught was approximately one half of the width. In the 1840's and 50's, the clippers were built entirely of wood. In the 1860's, they were sometimes built of wood but with iron frames.

KLIPPERSCHIFF
Drei Masten, alle mit Rahsegeln. Sie wurden für schnelles Ozeansegeln gebaut – mit Goldgräbern und Waren von der Ostküste der USA nach Kalifornien, später auch nach Australien; mit Tee und Gewürzen von China nach England. Die Klipperschiffe hatten einen stark nach vorne ragenden Steven, und die größte Breite des Rumpfes lag weiter nach achtern als bei anderen vergleichbaren Schiffen. Die Länge war mindestens fünfmal so groß wie die Breite und der Tiefgang war ungefähr die Hälfte der Breite. In den Jahrzehnten 1840 und 1850 wurden die Klipperschiffe voll aus Holz gebaut. Ab 1860 wurden sie auch mit dem Rumpf aus Holz und den Spanten aus Eisen gebaut.

NAVIRE CLIPPER
Les trois mâts ont tous des voiles carrées. Ils étaient construits pour des traversées rapides - avec des chercheurs d'or ou des marchandises de la côte Est des Etats-Unis vers la Californie, plus tard vers l'Australie, ou avec du thé et des épices de Chine vers l'Angleterre. Les clippers avaient une poupe proéminente, et le maximum de largeur de coque était plus en arrière que sur des bateaux comparables. La longueur était égale à au moins cinq fois la largeur et le tirant d'eau avait approxi-mativement la moitié de la largeur. Dans les années 1840 et 1850, les clippers étaient construits entièrement en bois.

SCHOONER

Two, sometimes three or more, equally tall masts, all carrying gaff sails. In rare cases, up to seven masts. Some square sails might be carried on the foremast. A ship with gaff sails is easier to handle than a square-rigged ship, so the crew could be somewhat smaller. A ship with gaff sails also tacks more easily than a square-rigger. Thus schooners were best in littoral waters with varying wind directions. Nineteenth century pleasure boats were often rigged as schooners. The most famous schooner is « America », built in 1851, the ship that lent its name to the most coveted sailing trophy in the world - America's Cup.

SCHONER

Zwei ungefähr gleich hohe Masten, beide mit Gaffelsegeln geriggt. Ein Schoner konnte aber auch Rahsegel auf dem vorderen Maste haben. Bis zu sieben Masten waren möglich. Ein Schiff mit Gaffelsegeln ist leichter zu handhaben als ein Schiff mit Rahsegeln. Die Mannschaft konnte daher kleiner sein als bei Rahsegeln. Ein Schiff mit Gaffelsegeln kreuzt auch besser als eines mit Rahsegeln. Die Schoner waren deshalb am besten für Küstengewässer mit wechselnden Winden geeignet. Im 19. Jahrhundert wurden Vergnügungsschiffe oft als Schoner getakelt. Der bekannteste Schoner ist die America, gebaut 1851. Sie gab dem begehrtesten Pokal der Segelsports den Namen - America's Cup.

GOELETTE

Deux mâts, parfois trois ou plus, les mâts avaient la même hauteur, tous ayant des voiles de flèche. Quelques voiles carrées pouvaient être établies sur le mât principal. Un bateau avec des voiles de flèche est plus rapide à manœuvrer qu'un voilier à voiles carrées, c'est ainsi que l'équipage pouvait être réduit. Un bateau avec des voiles de flèche remonte mieux et plus facilement au vent qu'un voilier à voiles carrées. De cette façon, les goélettes étaient les meilleures le long des eaux du littoral, avec des vents variables. Les bateaux de plaisance au 19è siècle étaient gréés en goélette.

BRIGANTINE

Two masts with square sails on the foremast and gaff sails on the second mast (mainmast). A brigantine was about the same size as a brig, but needed a smaller crew, as the gaff sail on the mainmast was easier to handle than square sails. They were used both in coastal waters and on the high seas. The square sails made the brigantine better suited than the traditional schooners for sailing in following winds.

BRIGANTINE

Zwei Masten mit Rahsegeln auf dem vorderen (Fockmast) und Gaffelsegel auf dem hinteren (Großmast). Eine Brigantine war ungefähr so groß wie eine Brigg, konnte aber eine kleinere Besatzung haben, weil das Gaffelsegel am Großmast leichter zu hantieren war als ein Rahsegel. Sie wurde sowohl in Küstengewässern als auch auf offenem Ozean eingesetzt. Durch die Rahsegel war eine Brigantine besser geeignet unter dem Wind zu segeln als die traditionellen Schoner.

BRIGANTINE

Deux mâts à voiles carrées sur le mât de misaine et voiles de flèche sur le grand mât. Une brigantine était à peu près de la même taille qu'un brick, mais nécessitait un équipage plus réduit, comme la voile de flèche sur le grand mât était plus facile à manier. Elles étaient toutes les deux hissées le long des côtes et en pleine mer. La voile carrée faisait que la brigantine allait mieux que les traditionnelles goélettes aux allures portantes.

BRIG

Two masts, both carrying square sails. A middle-size ship, generally used for freighting cargoes over large bodies of water, where following winds could be expected. A brig could fairly easily be manoeuvred under sail in restricted spaces. That made it well suited for voyages to small harbours where there were no tugs. The square sails, however, required a large crew.

BRIGG

Zwei Masten, beide mit Rahsegeln. Ein mittelgroßes Schiff, gewöhnlich für Reisen über große Strecken eingesetzt, auf denen man vor dem Wind segeln konnte. Eine Brigg konnte auch auf relativ kleinem Raum unter Segel manövriert werden. Sie wurde deshalb oft für Fahrten zu kleinen Häfen eingesetzt, in denen es keine Schlepper gab. Die Rahsegel erforderten allerdings eine relativ große Besatzung.

BRICK

Deux mâts, chacun portant des voiles carrées. Un bateau de taille moyenne, généralement utilisé pour transporter du fret à travers de larges étendues d'eau, où des vents portants pouvaient être attendus. Un brick pouvait être manoeuvré assez facilement sous voile dans des espaces réduits. Cela le rendait bien adapté pour des trajets vers de petits ports où il n'y avait pas de remorquage possible. Mais les voiles carrées exigeaient cependant un équipage plus important.

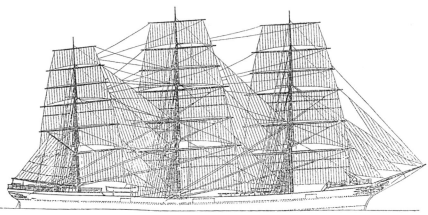

BARQUENTINE

Three or more masts with square sails on the foremast and gaff sails on the others. A middle-size ship which often sailed Northern European waters with variable winds. They were used in the lumber trade from Scandinavia to Germany and England across the Baltic and North Seas. A barquentine had a simpler rig than a barque and thus required a smaller crew. However, it did not sail as well as a barque in following wind.

BARKENTINE

Drei oder mehr Masten mit Rahsegeln auf dem vorderen Masten (Fockmast) und Gaffel- segeln auf den übrigen. Ein mittelgroßes Schiff, das oft auf nordeuropäischen Gewässern in wechselnden Winden segelte. Die Barkentinen transportierten Holz aus Skandinavien nach Deutschland und England über die Ostsee und die Nordsee. Sie hatten eine einfachere Takelung als eine Bark und kamen deshalb mit einer kleineren Besatzung aus. Allerdings segelte sie von dem Wind nicht so gut wie eine Bark

BARQUENTINE

Trois mâts ou plus avec des voiles carrées sur le mât de misaine et des voiles de flèche sur les autres. Un bateau de taille moyenne qui naviguait souvent dans les eaux nord européennes aux vents variables. Ils étaient utilisés pour les trafics de marchandises encombrantes depuis la Scandinavie vers l'Allemagne et l'Angleterre à travers la mer Baltique et la mer du Nord. Une barquentine avait un gréement plus simple qu'une barque et demandait ainsi un équipage plus restreint. Il ne naviguait cependant pas aussi bien qu'une barque aux allures portantes.

FULL-RIGGED SHIP

Three, four or in exceptional cases five masts with square sails on all masts. The clippers were full-rigged, but in the latter part of the 19th century, this ship type went through a development to reduce the number of men required. Hulls, masts and yards were made of iron or steel and sail handling was simplified. That made work aloft easier, and it was easier to adjust the sail area for various wind forces. The full-riggers were best suited for sailing in following winds. Thus, they were mainly used for intercontinental voyages in trade winds and monsoons.

VOLLSCHIFF

Drei, vier, in Ausnahmefällen fünf Masten mit Rahsegeln auf allen Masten. Die Klipper- schiffe waren Vollschiffe, aber im späteren Teil des 19. Jahrhunderts wurde dieser Schiffstyp weiterentwickelt, um die Mannschaftsstärke zu verringern. Schiffskörper, Masten und Rahen wurden aus Eisen oder Stahl gefertigt und die Handhabung der Segel wurde vereinfacht. Das machte die Arbeit in der Takelage einfacher, und es war leichter, die Segelfläche an unterschiedliche Windstärken anzupassen. Die Vollschiffe waren am besten für das Segeln unter dem Wind geeignet und wurden daher auf langen Strecken zwischen den Kontinenten im Passat und Monsun eingesetzt.

GRAND VOILIER A VOILES CARRÉES

Trois, quatre ou exceptionnellement cinq mâts à voiles carrées sur tous les mâts. Les clippers étaient tout équipés, mais dans la dernière partie du 19 ème siècle, ce type de bateau fût transformé pour réduire le nombre d'hommes nécessaires. Coques, mâts et vergues étaient en fer ou en acier et le maniement des voiles étaient simplifié. Cela rendait le travail dans la mâture plus facile, et il était plus simple de régler la voile selon la force du vent. Les voiles carrées fonctionnaient mieux pour les allures portantes. Aussi ils étaient principalement utilisés pour les voyages intercontinentaux dans les alizés et les vents de mousson.

THE STAR CLIPPERS FLEET

The *Star Flyer* and her sister ship *Star Clipper* are four-masted barquentines. The barquentines of the old days had gaff sails on the aftermost masts, but *Star Flyer* and *Star Clipper* instead carry more modern and easier-to-handle staysails on these masts. Hulls, masts and yards are made of steel, and the ships are built in Ghent, Belgium. They first set sail in 1991 and 1992, respectively. The *Royal Clipper* is a five-masted full-rigger. She was built of steel in Rotterdam, Netherlands, and was launched in 2000. The *Royal Clipper* is one of the biggest sailing ships ever built.

DIE STAR CLIPPERS FLOTTE

Star Flyer und das Schwesterschiff *Star Clipper* sind Viermastbarkentinen. In früheren Zeiten hatten die Barkentinen Gaffelsegel an den hinteren Masten, aber *Star Clipper* und *Star Flyer* haben stattdessen moderne und leichter zu bedienende Stagsegel an diesen Masten. Rumpf, Masten und Rahen sind aus Stahl. Die Schiffe wurden in Gent, Belgien gebaut. Sie setzten 1991 bzw. 1992 zum ersten Mal Segel. *Royal Clipper* ist ein Fünfmastvollschiff. Sie wurde in Rotterdam, Holland aus Stahl gebaut und lief im Jahre 2000 vom Stapel. *Royal Clipper* ist eines der größten Segelschiffe, die je gebaut wurden.

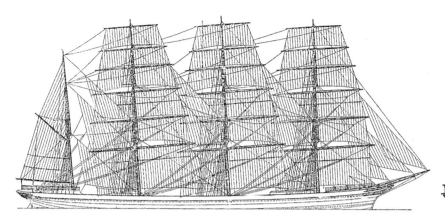

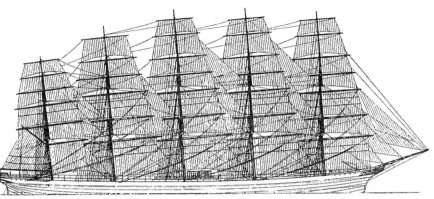

FOUR-MASTED BARQUE

Four masts, of which the fourth (jigger-mast) carried a gaff sail and the others square sails. From around 1900 and up to World War II, the four-masted barques were the most frequent sailing ships in the trans-oceanic trade. They could carry a great deal of cargo, and innovations in hull, rigging and equipment (e.g. steam-powered winches) made it possible to reduce the size of the crews. A frequent cargo was grain from Australia to Europe and nitrate and guano from the South American west coast. A few four-masted barques still sail as training vessels, e.g the Russian Kruzenshtern (built in 1926 as the Padua).

VIERMASTBARK

Vier Masten, von denen der hintere (Besanmast) ein Gaffelsegel hatte und die übrigen Rahsegel. Ab ungefähr 1900 bis zum Zweiten Weltkrieg waren Viermastbarken der häufigste Schiffstyp für lange Fahrten über die Ozeane. Sie konnten erhebliche Ladungen befördern und durch Vereinfachungen bei Schiffskörper, Takelage, und Ausrüstung (unter anderem dampfgetriebene Winden) konnte man mit einer relativ kleinen Besatzung auskommen. Typische Ladungen waren Weizen von Australien und Salpeter und Guano von der Westküste Südamerikas nach Europa. Einige Viermastbarken segeln noch als Schulschiffe, unter anderem die russische Kruzenshtern (1926 gebaut als die Padua).

QUATRE MÂTS BARQUE

Quatre mâts, dont le quatrième (tape-cul) portait une voile de flèche et les autres des voiles carrées. A partir de 1900 jusqu'à la deuxième guerre mondiale, les quatre mâts barque étaient des bateaux à voile, les plus nombreux, pour les trafics trans-océaniques. Ils pouvaient transporter un grand nombre de marchandises, et ils ont apporté de nombreuses innovations dans la coque, le gréement et divers équipements (par exemple les winches à vapeur) rendant possible la réduction de la taille des équipages. Une cargaison courante portait du blé d'Australie à l'Europe et des nitrates et du guano depuis la côte ouest de l'Amérique du Sud. Quelques quatre mâts barque naviguent toujours comme bateaux école, par exemple le Russe Kruzenshtern.

FIVE-MASTED FULL-RIGGER

Five masts, square sails on all masts. The first five-masted full-rigger was the Preussen, built in 1902 for the famous German Laeisz company. She was built for the nitrate trade from Chile to Germany and was then the biggest sailing ship ever built. The large sail area, 6,800 sq. metres (73,000 sq. feet) made her, in favourable circumstances, able to attain the same speed as the fastest clipper ships. For eight years, she sailed with great success. In 1910, the Preussen was accidentally rammed in the English Channel, drifted ashore and was wrecked near Dover. The Preussen was the only five-masted full-rigger built until Mikael Krafft and Star Clippers built the Royal Clipper in 2000.

FÜNFMASTVOLLSCHIFFE

Fünf Masten mit Rahsegeln an allen Masten. Das erste Fünfmastvollschiff war die Preußen, gebaut im Jahre 1902 für die berühmte deutsche Reederei Laeisz. Die Preußen wurde für den Transport von Salpeter von Chile nach Deutschland gebaut und war seinerzeit das größte je gebaute Segelschiff. Für acht Jahre segelte sie mit großem Erfolg. Im Jahre 1910 wurde die Preußen im Ärmelkanal gerammt, lief auf Grund und wurde in der Nähe von Dover zum Wrack. Die Preußen war das einzige Fünfmastvollschiff bis Mikael Krafft und Star Clippers im Jahre 2000 die Royal Clipper bauen ließen.

CINQ MÂTS CARRE

Cinq mâts, voiles carrées sur tous les mâts. Le premier cinq mâts à voiles carrées fut le Preussen, construit en 1902 pour la fameuse société allemande Laeisz. Il a été construit pour transporter le nitrate du Chili pour l'Allemagne et il a été le plus grand voilier jamais construit. Il a navigué avec grand succès pendant huit ans. En 1910, le Preussen a été accidentellement victime d'un abordage dans la Manche, il a dérivé à terre et il a fait naufrage près de Douvres. Le Preussen a été le seul cinq mâts à voiles carrées construit jusqu'à ce que Mikael Krafft et Star Clippers construisent le Royal Clipper en 2000.

LA FLOTTE DE STAR CLIPPERS

Le *Star Flyer* et *Star Clipper* sont des barquentines quatre mâts. Les barquentines des vieux temps avaient des voiles de pointes sur les mâts les plus en arrière, mais *Star Flyer* et *Star Clipper* portent à la place des voiles à poste fixe plus modernes et faciles à établir sur ces mâts. La coque, les mâts et les vergues sont en acier, et les bateaux ont été construits à Gand en Belgique. Les premières sorties ont eu lieu respectivement en 1991 et 1992. Le *Royal Clipper* est un cinq mâts carré. Il a été construit en acier à Rotterdam et il a été lancé en 2 000. Le *Royal Clipper* est l'un des plus grands voiliers jamais construit.

THE FIGUREHEAD of the
Royal Clipper.
Coin under the mast.

GALIONSBILD *auf der Royal
Klipper.*
Münze unter dem Mast

LA FIGURE *de proue du Royal
Clipper.*
Pièce de monnaie sous le mât.

OLD SAILORS' SUPERSTITIONS

Don't whistle.
Otherwise there will be a storm.
No umbrellas on board.
It means bad luck.
Flowers in soil.
Cause bad luck.
A priest dressed in black.
Means adverse wind.

Gambling with cards or dice.
Results in misfortune.
Black bags or suitcases.
Taboo on board.
**Never start a voyage on a
Friday.**
It will have a bad ending.

FOR GOD'S SAKE STOP WHISTLING

Men who follow the sea are the most superstitious lot of people on earth", writes Horace Beck in the book "Folklore and the Sea", published by the respected Mystic Seaport Museum in Mystic, Connecticut, USA. That is not true! There are other professions that are just as superstitious, like hunters and shepherds.

There is a scientific explanation. People who live close to unpredictable nature, yet depend on it, people who in their work are lonely, tired or anxious might want to look for security and try in various ways to predict danger and misfortune. Then they need old, well-tried knowledge, as well as magic and amulets. It was, and is, of vital importance for seamen to predict the weather. Today, there are reliable forecasts on radio and by satellite. Earlier, sailors had to observe the sky, waves, sun and moon. Their rules of memory were often rhymed.

If the sun sets clear as a bell,
It's going to blow sure as hell.
Red sun in the morning, sailors take warning
Red sun at night, sailor's delight.

But it might also be sheer magic. Many fishing boats around the world used to have - or still have - an eye painted on the bow. Larger sailing ships had a figurehead which was looking ahead and was said to be able to see dangers long before the look-out. A knock on the hull could wake up a sleepy look-out. The explanation given was that the figurehead or the Klabautermann, the brownie of the ship, had given a warning.

An earring is said to give the sailor good eyesight, and the old seaman's tattoo of a cross, an anchor and a heart (faith, hope and love) protects against dangers at sea and in port. Seaman Robert Stainsby, on Captain Cook's first voyage to Tahiti, was the first Westerner to undergo tattooing. More magic: A coin under the mast gives a ship fair winds and happy voyages. A cat on board will bring luck, but it has to be a ship's cat with six toes - not a normal five-toed cat.

For a cat to have six toes is a physical anomaly, called polydactylism. The most famous ship's cats live in the garden of Ernest Hemingway's house in Key West, Florida, today a museum. Hemingway got his first six-toed cat from a skipper. He named her Snowball, and she now has some 40 descendants. They live in the garden and are lovingly taken care of by museum staff. They drink water from a small fountain in the garden, actually a urinal, which Hemingway one wet night tore away at the infamous Sloppy Joe's Bar and carried home to his cats. Sea monsters, mermaids, ghost ships and Klabautermänner were realities of life for seamen. Some were dangerous, others helpful. It is unquestionable that seamen have actually seen sea monsters and creatures - there are too many accounts. But there is a scientific explanation.

Dr Glin Bennet at the University of Bristol in 1972 interviewed the 34 participants of a single-handed transatlantic yacht race. Most of them had had inexplicable experiences. But they hadn't seen monsters or Klabautermänner. One yachtsman describes how, after 56 hours at the helm, he discovered his father-in-law in the mast. Another competitor saw a small elephant having a splashing swim in the middle of the Atlantic. "A funny place to put a baby elephant", he thought and sailed on. Dr. Bennet sums up: "Sailors today see, hear and dream in the same way as sailors of bygone times when in the same situation. The difference only lies in the interpretation of the experience."

Seeleute sind die abergläubischsten Menschen auf der Welt" schreibt Horace Beck in dem Buch „Folklore and the Sea", das von dem angesehenen Mystic Seaport Museum in Mystic, Connecticut, USA, herausgegeben wurde. Das stimmt nicht! Es gibt andere Berufsgruppen, die genauso abergläubisch sind, so wie Jäger und Hirten.

Dafür gibt es eine wissenschaftliche Erklärung. Menschen, die nahe der unberechenbaren Natur leben und trotzdem auf sie angewiesen sind,

EVEN *in death, a tattooed cross shows that the seaman was a Christian and thus could be buried in the churchyard.*

EIN TÄTOWIERTES *Kreuz zeigte auch im Tode, dass ein Seemann Christ war und auf dem Kirchhof begraben werden konnte.*

MEME APRES *la mort, une croix tatouée montre que le marin était un Chrétien et devait être inhumé dans un cimetière.*

ALTER SEEMANNS ABERGLAUBE

Nicht pfeifen.
Es gibt sonst Sturm.
Keine Regenschirme an Bord.
Das bedeutet Unglück.
Blumen in Erde.
Verursachen Unglück.
Ein schwarz gekleideter
Priester. *Bedeutet Gegenwind.*
Karten- und Würfelspiele.
Bedeuten Unglück.
Schwarze Taschen.
Sind tabu an Bord,
Starte nie eine Reise an einem Freitag.
Sie wird schlecht ausgehen.

VIEILLES SUPERSTITIONS DE MARIN

Ne pas siffler.
Sinon il y aura une tempête.
Pas de parapluie à bord.
Cela porte malheur.
Fleurs en terre.
Provoque la malchance.
Un prêtre habillé en noir.
Veut dire vent contraire.
Jouer avec des cartes.
Entraine le malheur.
Des valises, des sacs noirs.
Sont tabous à bord.
Ne jamais commencer un voyage un vendredi.
Cela finira mal.

Menschen, die in ihrer Arbeit einsam, müde und voller Sorgen sind, suchen Sicherheit und versuchen auf unterschiedliche Art, Gefahren und Unglücke vorherzusehen. Dazu benötigen sie alte, erprobte Kenntnisse, aber auch Magie und Amulette. Für Seeleute war und ist es noch lebenswichtig, das Wetter vorauszusehen und zu vermeiden, von starken Winden überrascht zu werden. Heute gibt es verlässliche Vorhersagen im Radio oder durch Satelliten.

In früheren Zeiten mussten die Seeleute den Himmel, Wellen, Sonne und Mond beobachten. Die Gedächtnisstützen, die man sich schaffte, reimten sich oft, damit man sich leichter an sie erinnern konnte.

Sonne am Morgen bringt Kummer und Sorgen
Sonne am Abend, erfrischend und labend.

Aber es konnte sich auch um reine Magie handeln. Fischereifahrzeuge rund um den Globus hatten - und haben z.T. immer noch - ein Auge auf das Vorschiff gemalt.

Größere Segelschiffe hatten eine Galionsfigur, die nach vorn schaute und angeblich Gefahren lange vor dem Matrosen im Ausguck sehen konnte. Ein Krachen im Rumpf konnte so einen schläfrigen Ausguck wecken. Die Erklärung war, dass die Galionsfigur oder der Klabautermann die Warnung gegeben hatte.

Ein Ring im Ohr gibt dem Matrosen gutes Sehvermögen und die alte Tätowierung mit einem Kreuz, einem Anker und einem Herzen (Glaube, Hoffnung, Liebe) schützt vor Gefahren an Land und im Hafen.

Als erster Mann aus dem Westen ließ sich der Seemann Robert Stainsby tätowieren. Dies geschah während Kapitän Cooks erster Reise nach Tahiti.

Weiterer Aberglaube: Eine Münze unter dem Mast gibt dem Schiff guten Wind und glückliche Reisen. Eine Katze an Bord garantiert ebenfalls Glück; aber es muss eine Schiffskatze sein mit sechs Zehen - nicht fünf wie das für Katzen normal ist. Sechs Zehen sind eine Missbildung mit dem Namen Polydaktylie.

Die berühmtesten Schiffskatzen leben im Garten von Ernest Hemingways Haus in Key West, Florida. Heute ist das Haus ein Museum. Hemingway erhielt die erste sechszehige Katze von einem Schiffer. Er nannte sie Snowball und sie hat heute vierzig Nachkommen. Sie leben im Garten und werden von den Museumsangestellten liebevoll betreut.

Das Wasser trinken sie aus einem kleinen Brunnen im Garten, der eigentlich ein Urinal ist, das Hemingway während einer feuchten Nacht in der berüchtigten Bar Sloppy Joe's abmontierte und mit nach Hause zu den Katzen nahm.

Meeresungeheuer, Seejungfrau, Geisterschiff und Klabautermann waren auch Teil der Wirklichkeit für die Seeleute. Manche waren gefährlich, andere hilfreich. Es besteht kein Zweifel, dass Seeleute Untiere und Wesen wirklich gesehen haben. Die Berichte sind zu zahlreich.

Aber es gibt auch hier eine wissenschaftliche Erklärung. Dr. Glin Bennet von der Universität Bristol befragte im Jahr 1972 die 34 Segler, die an einem Einmann Wettbewerb über den Atlantik teilgenommen hatten. Die meisten hatten unerklärliche Erfahrungen gemacht. Allerdings hatten sie jetzt nicht Seeungeheuer oder den Klabautermann gesehen.

Ein Segler berichtete, dass er nach 56 Stunden am Ruder seinen Schwiegervater oben im Maste entdeckte. Ein anderer sah einen kleinen Elefanten mitten im Atlantik planschen und baden.

„Seltsamer Platz für einen kleinen Elefanten" dachte er für sich selbst und segelte weiter.

Dr. Bennet fasst zusammen: „Seeleute heute sehen, hören und träumen genauso wie Seeleute in früheren Zeiten, wenn sie sich in derselben Situation befinden. Der Unterschied liegt lediglich in der Deutung der Erfahrung."

CAPTURED albatrosses on the four-masted barque Beatrice, 1922.

GEFANGENE Albatrosse an Bord der Viermastbark Beatrice, 1922.

ALBATROS capturés sur un quatre-mâts barque, Beatrice, 1922.

Les marins sont les gens les plus superstitieux sur terre », a écrit Horace Beck dans le livre «Folklore and the Sea», publié par le respectueux Mystic Seaport Museum à Mystic, Connecticut, USA. Ce n'est pas vrai! Il y a d'autres professions qui sont aussi superstitieuses comme les chasseurs et les bergers.

Il y a une explication scientifique. Les gens qui vivent et dépendent de la nature parfois imprévisible, les gens qui travaillent seuls, qui sont fatigués ou anxieux qui recherchent la sécurité et essayent différents cheminements pour prévenir les dangers et les malheurs. Et puis ils ont besoin de connaissances anciennes reconnues, comme la magie et les amulettes. C'était et c'est d'une importance vitale pour les marins de prédire le temps et d'éviter d'être pris sans s'en rendre compte par des vents puissants.

Aujourd'hui, il y a des prévisions météorologiques exactes à la radio et par satellite. Auparavant, les marins devaient observer le ciel, les vagues, le soleil et la lune.

Soleil rouge le matin, les marins sont alertés.
Soleil rouge le soir, le délice du marin.

Mais ce peut être aussi de la pure magie. De nombreux bâteaux de pêche dans le monde entier, avaient - ou ont encore - un œil peint sur l'étrave. De plus grands voiliers avaient une figure de proue qui regardait vers l'avant et que l'on disait être capable de voir les dangers longtemps à l'avance. Un choc sur la coque pouvait réveiller un observateur endormi. L'explication donnée était que la figure de proue ou le Klabautermann, le lutin du bord, donnait l'alerte.

Il est dit que la boucle d'oreille donne bon œil au marin, et que le tatouage d'une croix sur un vieux marin, une ancre ou un cœur (foi, espérance et amour) protège contre les dangers en mer et au port. Le marin Robert Stainsby, sur le premier voyage vers Tahiti du Capitaine Cook, était le premier homme de l'ouest à se faire tatouer.

Plus de magie: Une pièce de monnaie sous le mât offre au bateau de bons vents et des voyages heureux. Un chat à bord apportera aussi la chance, mais il doit avoir six doigts de pieds et pas cinq doigts de pied comme un chat normal. Pour un

chat, avoir six doigts de pied est une anomalie physique, appelée polydactylisme.

Les chats de bateaux les plus célèbres vivent dans les jardins de la maison d'Ernest Hemingway au Key West, en Floride devenue, aujourd'hui un musée. Hemingway a eu son premier chat à six doigts de pied de la part d'un skipper. Il l'a appelé Snowbal, et il a maintenant quelques quarante descendants. Ils vivent dans le jardin et le personnel du musée en prennent soin. Ils boivent de l'eau d'une petite fontaine dans le jardin, autrefois un urinoir, qu'Hemingway lors d'une nuit pluvieuse arracha de l'infâme bar de Sloppy Joe et emporta à la maison pour ses chats.

Les monstres des mers, les sirènes, les bateaux fantômes et les lutins étaient des réalités de la vie pour les marins. Quelques-uns étaient dangereux, d'autres utiles. Il est indiscutable que les marins

aient effectivement vu des monstres marins et des créatures – ils sont trop nombreux à dénombrer.

Mais il y a une explication scientifique. Le Dr Glin Bennet de l'Université de Bristol en 1972 a interviewé les 34 participants d'une course transatlantique en solitaire. La plupart d'entre eux ont eu des expériences inexplicables. Mais ils n'ont pas vu des monstres ou des lutins.

Un plaisancier a dit qu'après 56 heures à la barre, il a découvert son beau-père dans le mât. Un autre concurrent a vu un petit éléphant pataugeant dans l'eau au milieu de l'Atlantique. « Un drôle d'endroit pour un bébé éléphant », se dit-il et poursuivit sa navigation. Le Dr Bennet résume: « Le marin d'aujourd'hui voit, entend et rêve de la même manière que les marins d'autrefois dans la même situation. La différence tient seulement dans l'interprétation de l'expérience. »

THE WANDERING *albatross is said to be the soul of a seaman.*

EIN WANDERALBATROS *soll die Seele eines Seemanns sein.*

IL EST DIT *que l'albatros errant est l'âme du marin.*

Beginning
of the End

STEAM ENGINE. *Propeller. Suez Canal. Panama Canal.*
Four steps. They meant the demise of the sailing cargo ships.

DAMPFMASCHINE. *Schiffsschraube. Suezkanal. Panamakanal.*
Vier Faktoren, die das Ende für die segelnden Frachtschiffe bedeuteten.

MACHINE À VAPEUR. *Hélice. Canal de Suez. Canal de Panama.*
Quatre étapes. Elles signifient la mort de la navigation commerciale à voile.

I n 1859, the steam ship *Ernst Merck* (picture) loaded guano in Rio de Janeiro. She was one of the first large steamers that had crossed the Atlantic, powered by a steam engine and a propeller, but also with the aid of sails. She was rigged as a barque. There was a strike in Rio de Janeiro, and the price of coal was high. In order to save money, the ship only bunkered coal for twelve days. The plan was to use sails for the rest of the voyage, which was expected to last for a little more than a month. But the voyage took almost twice that time.

When they were beginning to run out of water, the crew became desperate. Anything that could burn was used for firing under the boilers. Even parts of the rigging were used for firewood. She arrived in London in mid-December as a wreck. Her average speed during the voyage was less than four knots. As a comparison, the average speed of the clippers was close to seven knots.

The unhappy voyage of the *Ernst Merck* was typical of the first steamers. They were rarely faster than the sailing ships, until a web of coal bunkering stations had been established along the most important routes. The SS *Great Eastern*, the biggest steamer of her time and contemporary with the *Ernst Merck*, was also an economic failure. She could carry 4,000 passengers. On her maiden voyage across the Atlantic in 1860, only 35 persons wanted to, or dared, travel with her.

Nevertheless, it was the steam engine and the propeller which a few decades later would put the sailing merchant ships out of business.

The steam engine was developed by the Scotsman James Watt in the late 18th century, and in the early 19th century, paddle-steamers were used in coastal and inland waters. When the Swede John

A VICTORY FOR THE PROPELLER

On March 6, 1862, the *Monitor* steamed out of New York, headed for Hampton Roads. The Monitor was designed by the Swede John Ericsson and had a steam engine, a propeller and two guns. The American Civil War was ablaze, and little *Monitor* was the Union's response to the Confederate floating fortress *Merrimac*. "The *Monitor* looks like a pygmy compared to the *Merrimac*", wrote a crew member. The Battle of Hampton Roads went on for five hours. The American politician Robert Ingersoll wrote: "It was the guns of the *Monitor* that broke the fetters of four million slaves."

Ericsson patented an efficient propeller in 1836, the exposed and delicate paddle-wheels could be substituted. However there were many sceptics. A test was carried out on the Thames in the spring of 1837 in the presence of the British Lords Commissioners of the Admiralty. They were not impressed, and preferred the old paddle-steamers. So John Ericsson left England to seek his fortune in the United States. He had better luck there.

Im Jahre 1859 lag der Dampfer *Ernst Merck* in Rio de Janeiro und lud Guano. Es war eines der ersten großen Dampfschiffe, das den Atlantik mit Hilfe einer Dampfmaschine und Schiffsschraube überquert hatte, wobei man aber auch die Segel zu Hilfe nahm. Sie war als Bark getakelt. In Rio herrschte gerade Streik und der Preis für Kohle war hoch. Um zu sparen, bunkerte das Schiff lediglich für 12 Tage. Den Rest der Reise, die man mit gut einem Monat berechnet hatte, plante man zu segeln.

Die Fahrt dauerte dann aber fast doppelt so lange. Als die Wasservorräte an Bord zu Ende gingen, griff unter der Besatzung die Verzweiflung um sich. Sie nahmen alles Brennbare, um Feuer unter den Kesseln zu halten. Sogar Teile der Takelage wurden zu Feuerholz zerhackt. Die *Ernst Merck* kam Ende Dezember als Wrack in London an. Ihre Durchschnittsgeschwindigkeit während der Reise war knapp vier Knoten. Im Vergleich lag der Durchschnitt bei den Klipperschiffen fast bei sieben Knoten.

Die unglückliche Fahrt der Ernst Merck war typisch für die ersten Dampfschiffe. Sie waren selten schneller als die Segelschiffe, bis ein Netz von Bunkerstationen für Kohle längs der wichtigsten Handelsrouten eingerichtet war. Die *Great Eastern*,

damals größter Dampfer und zeitgleich mit der *Ernst Merck*, war ebenfalls ein wirtschaftlicher Misserfolg. Sie hatte Platz für 4 000 Passagiere. Auf der Jungfernfahrt über den Atlantik brachten nur 35 Personen den Mut auf, mitzufahren.

Trotzdem waren es die Dampfmaschine und die Schiffsschraube, die ein paar Jahrzehnte später die segelnden Handelsschiffe verdrängen sollten. Die Dampfmaschine wurde am Ende des 18. Jahrhunderts von dem Engländer James Watt erfunden und Anfang des 19. Jahrhunderts gingen Raddampfer in küstennahen Gewässern und Flüssen in Betrieb.

Als der Schwede John Ericsson 1836 ein Patent auf eine effektive Schraube erhielt, konnte das leicht zu beschädigende Schaufelrad der Dampfschiffe ersetzt werden. Viele waren allerdings skeptisch. Im Frühjahr 1837 wurde auf der Themse eine Probefahrt durchgeführt. Die anwesenden Lords der britischen Admiralität waren aber nicht beeindruckt sondern bevorzugten die alten Schaufelraddampfer. Daraufhin verließ John Ericsson England und versuchte sein Glück in den USA. Dort war er erfolgreicher.

En 1859, le bateau à vapeur *Ernst Merck* a chargé du guano à Rio de Janeiro. Il était l'un des premiers grands bateaux à vapeur qui a traversé l'Atlantique, propulsé par une machine à vapeur et une hélice, mais également avec l'aide de voiles. Il était gréé en barque. Il y avait une grève à Rio de Janeiro, et le prix du charbon était élevé. Afin d'économiser de l'argent, le bateau a mis en soute du charbon pour seulement 12 jours. L'idée était d'utiliser les voiles pour le reste du voyage qui devait prendre fin, un peu plus d'un mois plus tard. Mais le voyage prit

presque deux fois plus de temps. Quand il commençait à être à court d'eau, l'équipage devenait désespéré. Tout ce qui pouvait brûler était utilisé pour la chaudière. Même des morceaux du gréement étaient utilisés comme bois à brûler. Il arriva à Londres mi-décembre comme une épave. Sa vitesse moyenne pendant le voyage a été de moins de quatre nœuds. Par comparaison, la vitesse moyenne des clippers était proche de sept nœuds.

Le voyage malheureux du *Ernst Merck* était typique des premiers bateaux à vapeur. Ils étaient rarement plus rapides que les bateaux à voile, jusqu'à ce qu'un réseau de stations d'approvisionnement en charbon, ait été créé le long des routes maritimes les plus importantes. Le *Great Eastern*, le bateau à vapeur le plus grand de son temps et contemporain du *Ernst Merck*, était aussi un échec économique. Il pouvait transporter 4 000 passagers. Pour son voyage inaugural à travers l'Atlantique en 1860, seulement 35 personnes ont voulu, ou osé, voyager dessus.

De toute façon, ce sont les machines à vapeur et l'hélice, qui quelques décennies plus tard ont écarté les voiliers transporteurs de marchandise. La machine à vapeur a été développée par l'Écossais James Watt à la fin du 18è siècle et au début du 19è siècle, les bateaux à roues étaient utilisés le long des côtes et sur les eaux intérieures.

Quand le Suédois John Ericsson déposa un brevet hélice performante en 1836, les bateaux à aubes fragiles furent remplacés. Mais il y avait de nombreux sceptiques.

Un test a été organisé sur la Tamise en 1837 en présence des Commissaires des Lords britanniques de l'Amirauté qui préférèrent les vieux vapeurs à aubes. C'est ainsi qu'Ericsson quitta l'Angleterre pour faire fortune aux Etats - Unis. Il trouva là une meilleure chance.

THE STEAMSHIP
Ernst Merck, 1859, had a propeller, but sails as well.

DAS DAMPFSCHIFF
Ernst Merck, 1859, wurde von einer Schiffsschraube aber auch von Segeln angetrieben

LE NAVIRE A VAPEUR
Ernst Merck, 1859, avait une hélice, et naviguait également à la voile.

EIN SIEG FÜR DIE SCHIFFSSCHRAUBE

Am 5. März 1862 dampfte die *Monitor* von New York in Richtung Hampton Roads. Die Monitor war von dem Schweden John Ericsson konstruiert worden und hatte Dampfmaschine, Schiffsschraube und zwei Kanonen. Der amerikanische Bürgerkrieg war voll entbrannt und die kleine *Moni-*tor war die Antwort der Nordstaaten auf die schwimmende Festung *Merrimac* der Südstaaten. Fünf Stunden dauerte das Gefecht. Der amerikanische Politiker Ingersoll schrieb anschließend: „Es waren die Kanonen der Monitor, die die Fesseln von vier Millionen Slaven sprengten."

UNE VICTOIRE POUR L'HELICE

Le 6 mars 1862, le *Monitor*, est sorti de New York à la vapeur pour Hampton Roads. Le *Monitor* a été dessiné par le suédois John Ericsson et il avait une machine à vapeur, une hélice et deux canons. La guerre civile américaine avait éclaté, et le petit *Monitor* était la réponse de l'Union à la forteresse de la flotte de la Confédération, le *Merrimac*. La Bataille durait depuis cinq heures et le politicien américain Robert Ingersoll écrivit:
« Ce sont les canons du Monitor qui ont cassé les chaînes de quatre millions d'esclaves. »

TWO SHORTCUTS KILLED THE CLIPPER

The world's most famous clipper, the *Cutty Sark*, was launched in 1869. She was doomed from the outset. The same year, 1869, saw the opening of the Suez Canal. Suddenly, a shortcut was opened between Europe and Asia with its tea, spices, silk… Everything that Europe was clamouring for and would pay anything for could now be carried by steamboats through the Suez Canal. The voyage by way of the Canal was quicker and could often follow a time-table. A comparison:

In 1873, the *Cutty Sark* carried a tea cargo from China to England. It took 117 days. An English steamship that left China at the same time arrived 27 days earlier after transiting the Suez Canal. The construction of the Suez Canal took ten years and 1 million people were involved - 120,000 died from diseases.

In spite of the enormous work required - and the number of dead - another giant canal project was started a few years later - a waterway through the Isthmus of Panama.

It was France that started the construction in 1880, but gave up after more than ten years because of the yellow fever, malaria, cholera and technical problems. It has been estimated that 22,000 people died.

In 1904, the work was resumed, but under the direction of the United States. Great investments were made to combat tropical diseases - yet some 5,500 persons died during the ten years of construction. The layout of the canal was partly changed, with locks and artificial lakes. The canal was inaugurated in 1914.

As with the Suez Canal, the construction of the Panama Canal meant that steamships took over many trades - but not all. Chilean saltpetre, used for fertilizer and gunpowder, was still carried under sail around Cape Horn to Europe. Fast voyages were no priority, and the owners did not have to pay the expensive canal fees.

Der berühmteste Klipper der Welt, *Cutty Sark*, lief 1869 vom Stapel. Sie war von der ersten Stunde an zum Scheitern verurteilt. Im gleichen Jahr wurde der Suezkanal eingeweiht. Plötzlich öffnete sich eine Abkürzung zwischen Europa und Asiens Tee, Gewürzen, Seide... Alles, was Europa verlangte und für das es jeden Preis bezahlte, konnte jetzt mit Dampfern via den Suezkanal transportiert werden.

Die Fahrt durch den Kanal war schneller und folgte oft einem Fahrplan. Zum Vergleich: *Cutty Sark* segelte im Jahre 1873 mit Tee von China nach England. Die Fahrt dauerte 117 Tage. Ein englischer Dampfer, der China zur gleichen Zeit verließ kam 27 Tage früher an, nachdem er den Suezkanal passiert hatte.

Der Bau des Suezkanals dauerte 10 Jahre mit dem Einsatz von 1,5 Millionen Arbeitskräften, von denen 120 000 an Krankheiten starben. Trotz des enormen Arbeitsaufwandes und der Anzahl von Toten begann nur ein paar Jahre später ein

THE SUEZ CANAL
a few years before the opening in 1869.

DER SUEZKANAL
kurz vor der Einweihung 1869.

LE CANAL DE SUEZ
quelques années avant l'inauguration en 1869.

weiteres gigantisches Kanalprojekt - ein Wasserweg durch die Landenge von Panama. Frankreich begann den Bau im Jahre 1880, gab aber nach gut 10 Jahren wegen Gelbfieber, Malaria, Cholera und technischer Probleme auf. Man schätzt, dass 22 000 Personen den Tod fanden.

1904 wurden die Arbeiten fortgesetzt, jetzt aber unter der Leitung der USA. Es wurden beträchtliche Summen in die Bekämpfung von tropischen Krankheiten investiert; trotzdem starben mehr als 5 500 Menschen über die weiteren 10 Jahre Bauzeit. Der Kanal bekam nun zum Teil einen anderen Verlauf mit Schleusen und künstlichen Seen. Er wurde 1914 eingeweiht. Der Bau des Panamakanals führte, genau wie der Suezkanal dazu, dass Dampfschiffe viele Transporte übernahmen, wenn auch nicht alle. Salpeter aus Chile, ein wichtiges Düngemittel und nötig für Schwarzpulver, wurde weiterhin mit Segelschiffen via Kap Horn nach Europa befördert. Hier war nicht der schnelle Transport entscheidend und zusätzlich sparten sich die Reedereien die teuren Kanalgebühren.

Le plus célèbre clipper du monde, le *Cutty Sark*, fut lancé en 1869. Il connu une fin rapide dès l'ouverture du Canal de Suez en 1869. Très vite, un passage était crée entre l'Europe et l'Asie. Le thé, les épices, et la soie, tant convoités par l'Europe pouvaient alors être transportés par des bateaux à vapeur à travers le Canal de Suez. Un voyage beaucoup plus rapide. Par exemple:

En 1873, le *Cutty Sark* transportait une cargaison de thé de Chine en Angleterre. Cela prit 117 jours. Un vapeur anglais qui quitta la Chine en même temps arriva 27 jours plus tôt après avoir navigué à travers le Canal de Suez. La construction du Canal de Suez a duré dix ans et 1,5 millions de personnes y ont travaillé. Malgré un travail très difficile et environ 120 000 décès causés par des maladies - un autre projet gigantesque du canal a commencé quelques années plus tard. Une voie d'eau à travers l'isthme de Panama. La France commença la construction en 1880, mais abandonna, après plus de dix ans, à cause de la

fièvre jaune, la malaria, le choléra et des problèmes techniques. On compta 22 000 morts.

En 1904, le travail reprit, mais sous la direction des Etats-Unis. Des investissements importants ont été consacrés pour lutter contre les maladies tropicales - Cependant environ 5 500 personnes moururent pendant ces dix ans de construction. Le tracé du canal avait été partiellement modifié, avec des écluses et des lacs artificiels. Le canal a été inauguré en 1914.

Tout comme le Canal de Suez, la construction du Canal de Panama, augmenta le trafic et le transport par les bateaux à vapeur à quelques exceptions. Le salpêtre chilien, un engrais important, était encore transporté par les voiliers par le Cap Horn jusqu'en Europe. La rapidité des voyages n'était pas la priorité, et les propriétaires ne voulaient pas payer les droits de passage du Canal.

CONSTRUCTION of the Panama Canal, 1907.

DER PANAMA KANAL während des Baus im Jahre1907.

CONSTRUCTION du Canal de Panama , 1907.

THE CUTTY SARK, photographed by Captain Richard Woodget before 1916.

DIE CUTTY SARK, fotografiert von Kapitän Richard Woodget vor 1916

LE CUTTY SARK, phographié par le Capitaine Richard Woodget avant 1916.

A HATTER FROM HAMBURG

A young hat maker from Hamburg founded Germany's most famous shipping company - Laeisz. His name was Ferdinand Laeisz. Hat making in the 19th century was an extraordinarily dangerous profession. Large quantities of mercury went into the manufacturing of the felt for the hats. In 1824, the 23 years old Ferdinand Laeisz was pondering in the mercury fumes, thinking that the Germans who had emigrated to hot countries like Brazil, Argentina, Venezuela, Peru and Cuba would need his wide-brimmed hats. The first hat-laden ship left Hamburg the following year.

Surely, it is easy to associate his actions with the Mad Hatter in Lewis Carroll's "Alice's Adventures in Wonderland". His thoughts were devoid of any logic and his actions seemed mad.

But the Mad Hatter in Hamburg was right. A few years later, he could build the first ship of his own, the brig *Carl*, which sailed between Hamburg and South America. The ship was named after Ferdinand's son. Later, Carl's wife, Sophie, was the godmother of a ship with the strange name of *Pudel* (Poodle) - her nickname for her curly hair!

The *Pudel* was historic as the first ship in the Laeisz fleet with a name, beginning with P. That would later be a company trademark. Even today, the sixty-some ships run by the company all have names beginning with P.

The company already had its nickname "the Flying P-line" when *Pommern, Passat, Parma, Peking, Pamir, Padua, Preussen* and the other great sailing ships were carrying saltpetre - nitrate from Chilean ports to Europe. That was the toughest of all sailing ship trades. Sailing out to Chile, they had to round Cape Horn the wrong way - from east to west - against the westerly gales of the Roaring Forties.

Most often, the ships were four-masted barques, built of iron or steel to be able to withstand the extreme conditions. The largest ship in the Laeisz fleet was the five-masted full-rigger *Preussen*, built in 1902. According to the British maritime historian Alan Villiers, she was "not merely a beautiful ship and mind-boggling in terms of symmetry and seemingly weightless elegance, it was much more, it was as majestic as a queen. Those who saw it were rendered speechless."

Seamen nicknamed her "Queen of the Queens of the Seas". It is the *Preussen* which has served as the model for the world's second five-masted full-rigger - the *Royal Clipper*.

The *Preussen* was a real Flying P-liner, and it has been stated that she had been sailing at an average speed of almost 18 knots for twenty-four hours. Unfortunately, her sailing career lasted only eight years. In 1910, she was run into by a British steamer and drifted aground in Crab Bay near Brighton on the south coast of England. At low tide, parts of her hull are still visible.

At the outset of World War I, seven Flying P-Liners were loading saltpetre in Chilean ports - plus another 36 German sailing ships. They all remained in Chile for the duration of the war. In 1920-21, this sailing armada started its homeward voyage with a total cargo of 155,000 tons of saltpetre, or an average of 3,400 tons per ship. Saltpetre, or nitrate, was used as fertilizer and the demand in Europe was huge and the price was high.

According to the Versailles peace treaty, all German ships were to be handed over to the victorious powers, but Laeisz were allowed to sell the cargo. The sale was so profitable that Laeisz could buy back most of the fleet. In 1926, the last great sailing merchant ship - *Padua* - was launched. Then, the Laeisz company had been in existence for more than 100 years and owned a total of 86 sailing ships.

Ein Hutmacher aus Hamburg gründete Deutschlands berühmteste Reederei - Laeisz. Der Beruf des Hutmachers war im 19. Jahrhundert sehr gesundheitsgefährdend. Um den Filz für die Hüte herzustellen, wurden große Mengen an Quecksilber verwendet. Im Jahre 1824 kam dem 23jährigen Ferdinand Laiesz inmitten der Quecksilberdämpfe eine Idee. Könnten die deutschen Auswanderer in den warmen Ländern wie Brasilien, Argentinien, Venezuela, Chile, Peru und Kuba nicht meine breitkrempigen Hüte gebrauchen? Das erste Hut-Schiff verließ Hamburg im Jahr danach.

Gewiss kommt einem der Gedanke an den Hutmacher in Lewis Carrolls Alice in Wonderland; der Hutmacher, dessen Gedanken aller Logik entbehren und dessen Taten ungemein verrückt sind.

Aber der verrückte Hutmacher aus Hamburg sollte recht behalten. Nur ein paar Jahre später konnte er sein erstes eigenes Schiff bauen, die Brigg *Carl*, die zwischen Hamburg und Südamerika segelte. Das Schiff war nach Ferdinands Sohn benannt. Carls Frau Sophie wurde später Taufpatin für ein Schiff mit dem merkwürdigen Namen *Pudel* - das war ihr Kosename, wegen ihrer lockigen Haare! Das Schiff *Pudel* sollte historische Bedeutung erlangen; Es war das erste in der Laeisz Flotte, dessen Name mit dem Buchstaben P begann. Es sollte dann das Wahrzeichen der Reederei werden. Die rund 60 Schiffe, die die Reederei heute betreibt, haben alle den Anfangsbuchstaben P.

Den Rufnahmen Flying P-Line bekam die Reederei schon als die *Pommern, Passat, Parma, Peking, Pamir, Padua, Preußen* und andere Großsegler Nitrat von Häfen in Chile nach Europa beförderten. Dies war die schwierigste von allen Segelrouten. Auf dem Weg nach Chile mussten sie Kap Horn in der verkehrten Richtung umrunden - von Ost nach West - gegen die westlichen Stürme in den Roaring Forties (Heulenden Vierzigern).

Die Schiffe waren oft Viermastbarken aus Eisen oder Stahl, um mit den extremen Bedingungen fertig zu werden. Das größte Segelschiff in der Laeisz Flotte war das Fünfmastvollschiff *Preußen*, gebaut im Jahr 1902.

Der britische Marinehistoriker, Seemann und Verfasser Allan Villars beschrieb sie als „nicht nur ein schönes Schiff und atemberaubend mit seiner Symmetrie und schwereloser Eleganz, sie war soviel mehr, sie war majestätisch wie eine Königin. Jeder, der sie sah, war sprachlos."

Seeleute gaben ihr den Ehrentitel „Königin der Königinnen der Meere". Die *Preußen* war das Vorbild für das zweite Fünfmastvollschiff der Welt - *Royal Clipper*. Die Preußen war ein echter Flying P-Liner und soll angeblich an einem Tag mit einer Durchschnittsgeschwindigkeit von nahe 18 Knoten gesegelt sein. Um so schlimmer, dass sie nur acht Jahre segeln konnte. 1910 wurde sie von einem englischen Dampfschiff gerammt und lief in Crab Bay bei Brighton an Englands Südküste auf Grund. Bei Ebbe kann man immer noch Teile des Schiffsrumpfes sehen.

Bei Ausbruch des Ersten Weltkrieges lagen sieben P-Liner in verschiedenen chilenischen Häfen.

Außerdem ankerten dort noch weitere 36 deutsche Segelschiffe. Alle blieben während des Krieges in Chile. In den Jahren 1920-21 begann diese segelnde Armada die Heimfahrt nach Europa mit 155 000 Tonnen Salpeter. Salpeter wurde als Dünger verwendet; die Nachfrage war groß und der Preis hoch.

Alle deutschen Schiffe sollten, in Übereinstimmung mit dem Frieden von Versailles, an die Siegermächte übergeben werden, während die Ladung von der deutschen Laeisz verkauft werden durfte. Der Gewinn aus dem Verkauf war so groß, dass Laeisz den größten Teil der Flotte zurückkaufen konnte. Im Jahre 1926 lief der letzte große Handelssegler, die *Padua*, vom Stapel. Da bestand die Reederei Laeisz seit rund hundert Jahren und hatte insgesamt 86 Segelschiffe in ihrem Besitz gehabt.

Un jeune fabricant de chapeaux de Hambourg créa la plus célèbre société allemande de transport maritime - Laeisz. Son nom était Ferdinand Laeisz. Fabriquer des chapeaux au 19 ème siècle était une profession extrèmement dangereuse. Une grande quantité de mercure entrait dans la fabrication du feutre pour les chapeaux. En 1824, Ferdinand Laeisz âgé de 23 ans réfléchissait sur les fumées de mercure tout en pensant que les allemands, qui avaient émigrés vers des pays chauds tels que le Brésil, l'Argentine, le Vénézuéla, le Chili, le Pérou et Cuba, devraient avoir besoin de grands chapeaux.

Le premier bateau chargé de chapeaux quitta Hambourg l'année suivante. Il est facile d'associer les chapeliers à Lewis Carroll « Aventures d'Alice au pays des merveilles ». Ses pensées étaient dépourvues de la moindre logique et ses actions paraissaient démentes.

Mais le chapelier de Hambourg avait raison. Quelques années plus tard, il pouvait construire son premier bateau, le brick *Carl*, qui naviqua entre Hambourg et l'Amérique du Sud. Le bateau portait le nom du fils de Ferdinand. Plus tard, la femme de Carl, Sophie, était la marraine d'un bateau avec le nom étrange de *Pudel* (caniche) - son surnom en raison de sa coiffure frisée!

Le *Pudel* était historiquement le premier bateau de la flotte de Laeisz avec un nom commençant par P.

Même aujourd'hui, la soixantaine de bateaux gérés par la société ont tous des noms commençant par P. La société avait son surnom, la « Flying P. line ». A l'époque les *Pommern, Passat, Parma, Peking, Pamir, Padua, Preussen* transportaient du salpêtre du Chili vers les ports européens. C'était le cauchemar de tous de voiliers. Naviguer depuis le Chili, ils devaient contourner le Cap Horn dans le mauvais sens de l'est vers l'ouest - contre les coups de vent d'ouest des Quarantièmes Rugissants. Le plus souvent, les bateaux étaient des quatre mâts barques, construits en fer ou en acier pour être capables de résister aux conditions extrêmes.

Le plus grand bateau de la flotte de Laeisz était le cinq-mâts carré *Preussen*, construit en 1902. Selon l'historien maritime anglais Alan Villiers, il n'était « pas seulement un magnifique bateau et époustouflant en termes de symétrie et d'élégance. C'était bien plus, il était aussi majestueux qu'une reine et ceux que le voyaient restaient muets ». Des marins l'avait surnommé la « Reine des Reines des mers ».

C'est le *Preussen* qui servit de modèle pour le second plus grand voilier du monde, le cinq-mâts carré: le *Royal Clipper*.

Le *Preussen* était un réel Flying P. liner, qui pouvait naviguer à la vitesse moyenne de presque 18 nœuds pendant vingt-quatre heures. Malheureusement, sa courte carrière de voilier se termina huit ans plus tard. En 1910, il a été transformé par un armateur anglais en bateau à vapeur et il dériva sur la côte dans la Baie de Crab près de Brighton au sud de la côte anglaise. A marée basse, des morceaux de la coque sont encore visibles."

Au début de la Première Guerre Mondiale, sept Flying P. liners chargeaient du salpêtre dans les ports chiliens en plus de 36 autres voiliers allemands. Ils sont tous restés au Chili pendant la guerre. En 1920/1921 cet armada de voiliers commença son voyage de retour à la maison avec un total de 155 000 tonnes de salpêtre. Le salpêtre était utilisé comme engrais avec une forte demande en Europe et un prix élevé.

Selon le Traité de paix de Versailles, tous les navires allemands devaient être remis aux vainqueurs mais Laeisz fût autorisé à vendre ses cargaisons. La vente fût tellement profitable qu'il put racheter la plupart de sa flotte.

IN 1926, the last great sailing merchant ship - Padua - was launched.

IM JAHRE 1926 lief der letzte große Handelssegler, die Padua, vom Stapel.

EN 1926, le dernier grand voilier transporteur de marchandises - Padua - a été lancé.

SMALL ISLANDS BIG SHIPS

Åland is a little land of islands between Sweden and Finland. 5,000 islands, 30,000 inhabitants, 16 local government units and, astonishingly, 42 museums. It is a self-governing province within the Republic of Finland with a cabinet and prime minister of its own. As in all island states, the sea is always near.

In the 1930's Åland had the biggest sailing merchant fleet in the world. Most of the ships sailed under the white pennant of Gustaf Erikson. He was born in 1872 and went to sea at the age of ten. At 21, he had his own command, and in 1913, he founded a shipping company. He created his large fleet by buying second-hand tonnage cheaply, from Laeisz and others.

Now, saltpetre from Chile was no more the big deal, but wheat from Australia. Cheap, newly harvested wheat was loaded in Australia in January and sold in Europe in early summer, when the price was at its peak. That worked up to the outbreak of war in 1939.

In the 30's Gustaf Erikson's fleet was ever on the move, all over the world. Speed was not an important issue, and steam winches kept crew numbers low.

The *Pommern*, with a deadweight of 4,000 tons and 3,300 sq. metres (35,500 sq. feet) of sail on four masts was handled by 27 men. A steamer of equal size needed just as big a crew.

From the home port in Åland, the ships often sailed in ballast around the Cape of Good Hope eastward to Australia. They loaded in Port Augusta, Port Adelaide, Port Victoria or another of the small grain ports in the Spencer Gulf. Then, they continued on an easterly course, sailing with the wind in the Roaring Forties around Cape Horn and northward in the Atlantic to Europe.

The four-masted barque *Pommern*, one of Gustaf Erikson's ships, is now moored in Mariehamn as a museum ship.

It was the *Pommern* that Mikael Krafft, the owner of Star Clippers, saw as a young boy approaching Mariehamn alone in his little boat. It was there that he became infatuated with large sailing ships.

Åland ist ein kleiner Inselstaat zwischen Schweden und Finland, 30 000 Einwohner, 5 000 Inseln, ganze 16 Gemeinden und phänomenale 42 Museen. Es ist eine selbstverwaltete Provinz in Finland mit eigenem Staats- und Regierungspräsidenten. Wie in allen Inselstaaten ist das Meer ständig gegenwärtig.

In den dreißiger Jahren gab es in Åland die größte segelnde Handelsflotte. Die meisten Schiffe segelten unter der weißen Flagge von Gustaf Erikson. Dieser wurde 1872 geboren und ging als 10jähriger zur See. Mit 21 erhielt er sein erstes Kommando und 1913 gründete er seine eigene Reederei. Er baute eine Flotte von großen Schiffen auf, indem er billig einkaufte, unter anderem bei der deutschen Reederei Laiesz. Jetzt ging es nicht mehr um Salpeter sondern um Weizen aus Australien.

Billiger, frisch geernteter Weizen wurde im Januar in Australien geladen und im Frühsommer in Europa verkauft, wenn der Preis am höchsten war. Dies ging gut bis zum Kriegsausbruch 1939.

In den dreißiger Jahren war Gustaf Ericsons Flotte rund um den Erdball unterwegs. Die Schnelligkeit war nicht so wichtig und die Besatzung hielt man klein mit Hilfe von dampfangetriebenen Winden.

Die Pommern, mit 4 000 Tonnen Tragfähigkeit und 3 300m² Segelfläche auf vier Masten wurde mit 27 Mann gesegelt. Auf einem Dampfschiff vergleichbarer Größe benötigte man die gleiche Besatzung. Vom Heimathafen auf Åland ging die Reise oft mit Ballast rund um das Kap der Guten Hoffnung in Richtung Osten nach Australien. Geladen wurde in Port Augusta, Port Adelaide, Port Victoria oder einem anderen kleinen Weizenhafen im Spencergolf.

Dann nahm man wieder Kurs nach Osten, folgte den „Roaring Forties" rund um Kap Horn und segelte schließlich in Richtung Norden durch den Atlantik nach Europa. Die Viermastbark *Pommern*, eine von Gustaf Eriksons Schiffen, liegt heute als Museumsschiff in Mariehamn.

Es war die *Pommern*, die Mikael Krafft, Eigentümer der Star Clippers, sah, als er als Jugendlicher allein mit seinem kleinen Boot nach Mariehamn segelte. An dieser Stelle wurde er von den großen Segelschiffen inspiriert.

Åland est un petit pays composé d'îles, entre la Suède et la Finlande. 5 000 îles, 30 000 habitants et étonnamment, 42 musées. C'est une province autogouvernée au sein de la République de Finlande avec un cabinet et un premier ministre indépendants. Comme pour tous les états insulaires, la mer est toujours proche. Dans les années 1930, Åland avait la plus grande flotte marchande à voile au monde.

La plupart des bateaux naviguaient sous le drapeau blanc de Gustaf Erikson. Il était né en 1872 et navigua en mer à l'âge de dix ans. A 21 ans, il était son propre commandant, et en 1913, il fonda une société maritime. Il créa une grande flotte en achetant des bateaux d'occasions pas chers à Laeisz et à d'autres. Le salpêtre du Chili devint moins important et le trafic du blé d'Australie augmenta. Bon marché, juste moissonné, le blé était embarqué en Australie en janvier et vendu en Europe au début de l'été quand le prix était à son sommet. Cela fonctionna jusqu'à l'éclatement de la guerre de 1939. Dans les années 30 la flotte de Gustaf Erikson était toujours en mouvement dans le monde entier. La vitesse n'était pas un but majeur et les winches à vapeur permettaient de garder un équipage réduit. Le *Pommern*, avec un poids à vide de 4 000 tonnes et une voilure de 3 300 m² dans les quatre mâts était mené par 27 hommes. Un bateau à vapeur d'une taille identique avait besoin d'un équipage aussi important.

Depuis le port d'attache à Åland, les bateaux naviguaient souvent avec du lest autour du Cap de Bonne Espérance vers l'est jusqu'en Australie. Ils embarquaient dans les petits ports leurs cargaisons de blé du Golfe de Spencer.

Ensuite, ils continuaient vers l'est, naviguant avec le vent dans les Quarantièmes Rugissants, par le Cap Horn et puis vers le nord dans l'Océan Atlantique, vers l'Europe.

Le quatre-mâts barque *Pommern*, l'un des bateaux de Gustaf Erikson, est maintenant amarré à Mariehamn comme bateau musée. C'est à bord de son petit bateau approchant Mariehamn, que Mikael Krafft, aujourd'hui propriétaire du Star Clippers, découvrit dès son plus jeune âge et pour la première fois le *Pommern*. Ce fût alors le début de sa passion pour les grands voiliers.

THE POMMERN *was opened as a museum ship in Mariehamn in 1957. The Pommern off Falmouth, England, in 1939.*

DIE POMMERN *wurde im Jahre 1957 in Mariehamn zum Museumsschiff Die Pommern im Jahre 1939 vor Falmouth in England*

LE POMMERN *est devenu un musée ouvert au public à Mariehamn en 1957. Le Pommern, au large de Falmouth, Angleterre, en 1939.*

Credits

THE AUTHOR

Erling Matz, writer and marine historian, has written or contributed to about 40 books. He was at one time the Information Manager at the Vasa Museum in Stockholm, Sweden.

Thank you Danke Merci

During the years I spent planning and making an inventory for this book, I was given invaluable help by a large number of amiable and skilful people.
Star Clippers and I would like to thank all the museums, libraries and archives that have helped me to realize this book.
That is people in the United Kingdom, USA, France, Germany and Holland -
and specifically the staff at the National Maritime Museums of Sweden (NMMS).
I would also like to thank captain Klaus Müller, Star Clippers, Karin Gautier and sailing friend David Campbell for facts and translation checking.
Although every effort has been made to trace and contact copyright holders, in a few instances this has not been possible.
If notified, the publisher will be pleased to rectify any omission in future editions.
Erling Matz February 2013